The Roman Predicament

The Roman Predicament

HOW THE RULES OF INTERNATIONAL

ORDER CREATE THE POLITICS OF EMPIRE

Harold James

PRINCETON UNIVERSITY PRESS
PRINCETON AND OXFORD

Copyright © 2006 by Princeton University Press

Published by Princeton University Press, 41 William Street, Princeton, New Jersey 08540

In the United Kingdom: Princeton University Press, 6 Oxford Street, Woodstock, Oxfordshire OX20 1TW

Second printing, and first paperback printing, 2008

Paperback ISBN: 978-0-691-13635-6

The Library of Congress has cataloged the cloth edition of this book as follows

James, Harold, 1956–

The Roman predicament : how the rules of international order create the politics of empire / Harold James.

p.   cm.

Includes bibliographical references and index.

ISBN-13: 978-0-691-12221-2 (cl : alk. paper)

ISBN-10: 0-691-12221-0 (cl : alk. paper)

1. Imperialism.   2. Power (Social sciences)   3. International economic relations.
4. International organization.   5. Social values.   6. Rome—History—Empire,
30 B.C.–476 A.D.   7. Smith, Adam, 1723–1790. Inquiry into the nature and causes
of the wealth of nations.   8. Gibbons, Edward, 1737–1794. History of the decline and
fall of the Roman Empire.   I. Title.

JC359.J35 2006

325'.32—dc22   2005055080

British Library Cataloging-in-Publication Data is available

This book has been composed in Minion Typeface

Printed on acid-free paper. ∞

press.princeton.edu

Printed in the United States of America

10   9   8   7   6   5   4   3   2

Contents

Acknowledgments

I SHOULD LIKE TO THANK Niall Ferguson, Marzenna James, and John Ikenberry, as well as the reviewers for Princeton University Press, for their careful reading of the manuscript and illuminating suggestions; and Peter Dougherty for his editorial support and encouragement, as well as Sophia Efthimiatou and Linda Truilo of Princeton University Press for their help with the preparation of the manuscript. John Ikenberry's Georgetown and then Princeton discussion group on national security challenges was also a source of inspiration for some of the themes and ideas explored in the following pages. I have also benefited from being able to present the themes of the book at lectures and seminars for CES-IFO, Munich; the Federal Reserve Bank of Dallas; the Foreign Policy Research Institute, Philadelphia; the German Historical Institute, Washington, D.C.; the Herbert-Quandt-Stiftung, Bad Homburg; the National Intelligence Council's 2020 Project; and Schloss Elmau, Bavaria. I should also like to thank the German Historical Institute in Washington for allowing me to reuse in chapters 3 and 4 some of the material previously used in their *Bulletin*.

The Roman Predicament

Introduction

Modern America is strangely fascinated with imperial Rome. Our Capitol, and our best train stations, look Roman. Roman and classical images surface in popular culture at regular but not chance intervals: the big films of the 1950s and 1960s, from *Ben Hur* (1959), *Spartacus* (1960), *Cleopatra* (1964), and *Fall of the Roman Empire* (1964) were also films of the Cold War, in which the imperial analogy looked very attractive. The classical blockbuster then stopped quite suddenly, however, with Vietnam-era doubts. The idea revived with *Gladiators* (2000), or *Troy* (2004) and *Alexander* (2004). Classical empires literally speak to us—but they require some interpretation.

This book is about what I term the "Roman dilemma": the way in which peaceful commerce is frequently seen as a way of building a stable, prosperous, and integrated international society. At the same time, the peaceful liberal economic order leads to domestic clashes and also to international rivalry and even wars. The conflicts disturb and eventually destroy the commercial system and the bases of prosperity and integration. These interactions seem to be a vicious spiral, or a trap from which it seems almost impossible to escape. The liberal commercial world order subverts and destroys itself.

The central problem is that we need rules for the functioning of complex societies, whether on a national (state) level or in international relations. We do not, however, always comply voluntarily with rules, and rules require some enforcement. In addition, rules need to be formulated. The enforcement and the promulgation of rules are both consequences of power, and power is concentrated and unequally distributed. Even when we think of voluntarily negotiated rules, there is the memory of some act of power, the long shadow of a hegemonic strength—the shadow of Rome—falling on the negotiators. The propensity for subversion and destruction of a rule-based order comes about whenever there is a perception that rules are arbitrary and unjust, and that they reflect the imposition of particular interests in a high-handed imperial display of power.

Power protects commerce and peace, but power is clearly not necessarily a good in itself. It offers a basis on which there occurs a constant accumulation of greater power, as power is used to affect the outcome of social processes. One way of putting this is the frequently made observation that the exercise of power has an addictive quality. The adage that power tends to corrupt itself affects the way in which the holders of power behave. Even if the wielder of power resists the addiction, other people suspect the addiction.

Rules guide conduct at both national and international levels, and a central theme of the book is the interdependence of the rule systems on both levels. The book's goal is to bring together debates that are normally conducted separately, the separation of which has frustrated many analysts. Helen Milner recently complained that "one could caricature International Relations by saying that those who study security policy emphasize state actors, and those who study political economy focus more on societal actors."[1] Such a scholarly division of labor may make sense in terms of academic tradition, but scholars working according to this division are missing the complexities of a world in which minds shift continually from one area of concern to another, and in which policies are made in the light of such shifts.

The following essay examines the mental maps that shape our response to the confusion about the relationship of power to the rules we see around us. The fragility of order is a theme that has exercised much of the recent discussion in International Relations. Liberal internationalists are concerned with the difficulties of making and maintaining an open international order, while realists see the story in terms of tragic clashes.[2] Both approaches could benefit from a historical understanding of the way in which visions of order come about.

The imperial analogy has for long been one of the most attractive ways of understanding and criticizing political and economic power when such power appears threatening or arbitrary. The search for a predecessor or a model goes back even further than Rome. Ancient Romans were gripped by the image of Alexander the Great, and some of the most charismatic rulers actively sought an *imitatio Alexandriae*. Yet often the model is a negative rather than a positive one. In the eighteenth century, for example, when the United States was founded in a revolt against imperial rule, the Roman analogy dominated discussion. The historical image offered a parallel to a quest for certainty and a demand for rules as a condition of justice.

The book begins with an examination of two very famous books on the subject, both by chance published in the same year, 1776—a year that produced not only the U.S. Declaration of Independence but also the first extensive elaborations of the debate about commerce and domination, drawing explicit lessons from the Roman experience: *The Wealth of Nations* and *The Decline and Fall of the Roman Empire*. Adam Smith and Edward Gibbon wrote studies that became instantly celebrated, and whose basic ideas are still a familiar tool of debates in the twenty-first century. Most educated people today recognize a very simple set of ideas associated with Smith and Gibbon, even if they have never read these multivolume products of high eighteenth-century scholarship in their entirety (in the same way as Marx, Nietzsche, Freud, or Keynes seem familiar to all of us). In this caricatured interpretation, Smith defended (or even invented) the free market; and Gibbon blamed monks for the fall of Rome. One of the goals of this book is to set out the surprising (and in some aspects quite unfamiliar) aspects of the complementary analyses presented in the *Wealth of Nations* and in the *Decline and Fall of the Roman Empire*. Smith and Gibbon were both concerned with the internal logic that eroded great accumulations of power. The authors of 1776 offered a package that is more alluring, and more relevant to our current debates, than the constructs of the later iconic thinkers.

Smith and Gibbon were gloomy about imperial systems and saw decay and doom. Some of the doom was straightforwardly economic, since fiscal overextension was an obvious problem in the maintenance of an imperial order. The eighteenth-century writers also invited their readers to think about the difficulties inherent in sustaining a common set of values over a vast territory and a diverse population.

This study then (chapter 2) goes on to analyze in turn the fluctuating and occasionally ideological ways in which integration and globalization are seen by participants, policymakers, and critics. Does a globalized world need a single authority first to formulate and then enforce rules? Where does the legitimacy of the rules come from? Does a system of rules presuppose the elaboration of a value system? How is that value system derived, or is it necessarily imposed by an act of power? Is there a necessary tension between rules and power? Globalization requires rules that are formulated and elaborated in what might be termed "power centers." There is a continuous instability, however, that makes for problems. Inequality can lead to challenges against the rule-making process; so does a diversity of tastes and cultures. The imperial analogy is a good or at least an easily available way of describing the development of power on the basis of inequality and its use to suppress cultural diversity. The inherent fragility lies in that whenever we interpret the rules that should guide our conduct as being part of a conspicuous exercise in imperial power, we are more likely to revolt.

The next chapter (3) then examines three areas of debate about the international economy today in which the tension between rules and power is particularly intense: the world trading system, the governance of corporations, and the international monetary order. A further chapter (4) is concerned with the sustainability of U.S. power in the modern world, and offers reflections on whether analogies with British power in the eighteenth century or Roman power in the ancient world are appropriate. Chapter 5 turns to conflict. How do international conflicts and wars—both small and big—affect the balance of perception between rule and arbitrariness? Chapter 6 looks at the tensions between center and periphery in imperial systems or systems of power. Empires seem most fragile in a historical survey at their most remote outposts. Does remoteness have the same meaning in a modern world with much higher levels of interconnectedness and with instantaneous communication? Finally Chapter 7 investigates the only model that is currently suggested as an alternative to the traditional idea of power: the apparently attractive idea that there might be a way of breaking out of the eternal yin and yang between rule and rulelessness. Europeans sometimes think that they have discovered in a new form of supranational management—the European Union—a new clue to stability that eludes the United States, which is trapped in the predicaments of being a superpower: in other words, in the Roman predicament.

Finally, the conclusion investigates another tradition of thinking about order, as part of a natural law basis for a global society. Might this offer a way out of the trap that Smith and Gibbon analyzed with such acuity at the time of the founding of the American republic? Or is the slide from republic to empire an inevitable one? The problem that the natural law tradition seeks to overcome is the dependence of alternative visions on examinations of the processes involved in rule rather than the underlying moral and ethical basis. A discussion of values, rather than debate over procedures, is an eighteenth-century solution to the problem, a solution that also has an appeal in the twenty-first century.

This is not a book on globalization, which has produced a vast literature; nor is it a book on empire and whether the United States is or should be considered as an empire, on which there is also by now a rapidly expanding but often polemical and superficial literature. This book tries to place recent debates in a deeper historical and economic perspective: in my view, the problem with most books on foreign strategy debates (such as the recent works of Walter Russell Mead, Robert Kagan, or John Lewis Gaddis) is their almost total disregard of economic dimensions; while the books of imperial nostalgia (Niall Ferguson or Deepak Lal) or those attacking imperial revival (Chalmers Johnson, Andrew Bacevich, Emmanuel Todd, Michael Mann, to name but some of the most prominent) ignore important changes in the character of modern society and in the availability of knowledge that make our society quite different to that of past imperial societies.

There is, however, one constant that runs through these debates: it lies in the character of the relationship between social order and rules. That is the debate that Adam Smith in the *Wealth of Nations* and Edward Gibbon in the *Decline and Fall of the Roman Empire* opened in 1776 with a brilliance and intellectual clarity that has never since been surpassed.

The Model of Decline and Fall

O̶UR PREDECESSORS have thought about problems similar to those of the modern globalizing world, and they in turn believed that they could understand their environment by thinking about their own predecessors. Faced with an economic dynamism, that was both driven and divided by the assertion of political power, they saw the Roman Empire as a model for the dilemmas of future ages.

The discussion of the Roman predicament reached a high point in 1776, the year when discontent with British rule led to the American Declaration of Independence. On April 1, Edward Gibbon wrote to the Scottish philosopher Adam Ferguson, "What an excellent work is that with which our common friend, Mr. Adam Smith, has enriched the public!—an extensive science in a single book, and the most profound ideas expressed in the most perspicuous language."[3] In that year, in fact, the first volumes of two important books were published: Smith's *An Inquiry into the Nature and Causes of the Wealth of Nations*, and Gibbon's own *Decline and Fall of the Roman Empire*.[4] Both were instantly famous, and both eventually came to be appreciated more for remarkable passages in the most perspicuous language, rather than for the overall argument presented. The argument of neither work was entirely clear from the opening volumes, but when completed, they presented a parallel and rather gloomy account of the predicament of the imperial society in which they had been created.

The consensus of modern interpreters has made it an acceptable cliché that Edward Gibbon wrote as much about his own times as about the Roman Empire (commentators actually like to make this kind of claim of any major analyst of a completely different epoch). They have even inspired a reaction by self-appointed purists who want to reassert that Gibbon was really what he thought he was, namely first and foremost a historian.[5] Being a historian and reflecting on the present was for Gibbon, however, a parallel exercise, and he knew well that it was only through the choice of an appropriate subject that the historian could have influence, or indeed really be a historian. He initially considered a large number of possible subjects for a history, mostly of a biographic nature: Charles VIII of France, Edward the Black Prince, Henry V, or Sir Philip Sidney, or Sir Walter Raleigh. Each might have given rise to an interesting study, but none would have shaken the eighteenth-century world view or made Gibbon into the preeminent historian of his age. Gibbon also penned a history of the Swiss, which, when read aloud to a salon audience, was received with moderate interest and sympathy, and which was never published in his lifetime. Ancient Rome was the challenge that made Gibbon great and at the same time showed how Great Britain was less than great.

It is also clear that as Gibbon wrote his history, he was more and more held in the grip of a genuine and romantic passion for Rome, and he later provided a famous account of how the idea of the Roman history came:

> it was at Rome on the fifteenth of October 1764, as I sat musing amidst the ruins of the Capitol, while the barefooted friars were singing Vespers in the temple of Jupiter, that the idea of writing the decline and fall of the City first started to my mind.[6]

This retrospective account is wrong, however, not just pedantically (the modern church of Santa Maria in Aracoeli had not been a temple of Jupiter but rather of Juno Moneta), but more fundamentally, because it transposes the views of the late Gibbon onto the historical imagination of the young man. Recent commentators, especially David Womersley, have argued convincingly that while Gibbon ended as a "real" historical historian, and saw himself as such, he began much more as a characteristically eighteenth-century figure, a philosophical historian who would use the past as part of a general attempt to describe—in the manner of Montesquieu, to whom Gibbon owed a substantial debt—the political and social condition of a modern age. "The subject of history is man," he boldly concluded. Yet it actually takes little to work out what Gibbon was fascinated by in the 1770s.

Gibbon reflected on a common method by which the "eager trembling curiosity of mankind" wished to "penetrate into futurity": "Sometimes they have commenced prophets, and even true prophets at a very easy rate, by delivering the narrative of things already past under the name of some celebrated character of a distant age."[7] Virgil in this way used Aeneas and the Sibyl. The eighteenth-century author frowned upon the obvious impostor: on the other hand, he saw his exploration of Rome and the British Crown's dealings with North America as parallel exercises. He wrote to his friend Georges Deyverdun in the spring of 1776, "[F]rom the meeting of Parliament, when it became necessary to finish my book and to subdue America I found myself involved in a greater hurry of public private and literary business than I have ever known in any part of my life." Looking back later, he told Deyverdun that "in modern history there will always be some question of the decadence of Empires, and as far as I know from my memory you like the power of England as little as that of the Romans."[8]

At the same time that he was composing his history, Gibbon was following the affairs of America: indeed his foremost modern biographer has calculated that he acquired between 1770 and 1775—in other words, at the time that he was preparing the first volume of *Decline and Fall*—as many books on parliament and the American situation as on Rome.[9] By the end of 1775, he was describing the British empire in the same phrases he had for Rome:

> we shall find ourselves engaged in carrying out the most serious business, perhaps, that the Empire ever has known. A dark cloud still hangs over it, and though it may be necessary to proceed, the contest will be difficult, the event doubtful, and the consequence destruction.[10]

At frequent intervals, especially in the early volumes of the monumental history, Edward Gibbon laid down a heavy didacticism: history, he says, "undertakes to record the transactions of the past, for the instruction of future ages."[11] His readers quickly recognized the point. The wife of the Swiss financier Necker, Suzanne Necker, who knew Gibbon very well, saw Gibbon's achievement in "having filled an immense interval in history . . . having thrown over chaos this bridge that unites the ancient and the modern worlds."[12]

Edward Gibbon begins the *Decline and Fall* with an evocation of the peaceful character of the early Roman Empire, and of its prosperity. He begins by stating that

> the principal conquests of the Romans were achieved under the Republic. . . . Inclined to peace by his temper and situation, it was easy for [Augustus] to discover that Rome, in her present exalted situation, had much less to hope than to fear from the chance of arms; and that, in the prosecution of remote wars, the undertaking became every day more difficult, the event more doubtful, and the possession more precarious, and less beneficial. (I:1–2)[13]

Augustus's successors were just as peaceful, though not as a result of virtuous motives.

The empire moved away from the austere simplicity of the Roman Republic, because commercial society and spreading prosperity meant expenditure on conspicuous consumption rather than on arms. Emulation, the downward social dissemination of the fashionable and the ostentatious, was for Gibbon as much a characteristic of ancient Roman behavior as it was in his own time of ferociously consuming eighteenth-century Britons.

At first, much of the grandeur of Rome was the product of an imperial passion, for "Augustus was accustomed to boast that he had found his capital of brick, and that he had left it of marble" (I:39). Private citizens rapidly imitated the emperors in a lust for ostentatious consumption:

> But if the emperors were the first, they were not the only architects of their dominions. Their example was universally imitated by their principal subjects, who were not afraid of declaring to the world that they had spirit to conceive, and wealth to accomplish, the noblest undertakings. Scarcely had the proud structure of the Coliseum been dedicated at Rome, before the edifices, of a smaller scale indeed, but of the same design and materials, were erected for the use, and at the expense, of the cities of Capua and Verona. (I:39)

The commercialization of society depended on the rich, and on their desire to distinguish themselves by unique consumption patterns—which turned out to be very easily emulated.

The Roman revolution involved a move away from the more equitable distribution of property that had characterized the republican polity.

9

The shift to inequality, as has sometimes been noted, is distinctly parallel with the developmental paradigm as presented by Adam Smith.[14] Economic development, and the course of human history, has moved through successive stages. Settled agriculture and trade made for a permanent improvement in the condition of humankind, and commerce made possible civility:

> the same freedom of intercourse which extended the vices, diffused likewise the improvements of social life. In the more remote ages of antiquity, the world was unequally divided. The East was in the immemorial possession of arts and luxury; whilst the West was inhabited by rude and warlike barbarians, who either disdained agriculture, or to whom it was totally unknown. Under the protection of an established government, the productions of happier climates, and the industry of more civilised nations, were gradually introduced into the western countries of Europe; and the natives were encouraged, by an open and profitable commerce, to multiply the former, as well as to improve the latter. It would be almost impossible to enumerate all the articles, either of the animal or the vegetable reign, which were successively imported into Europe, from Asia and Egypt. (I:46)

Gibbon produced his own version of the famous early eighteenth-century Mandevillian fable of the bees, with its apparently amoral conclusion that private vices were public virtues. Bernard Mandeville had been roundly condemned by conventional Christian moralists for his attack on simple virtue; as indeed Gibbon would later be attacked for his apparent cynicism about Christianity. For Gibbon, the empire, and perhaps civilization in general, depended on luxury and consumption.

> Under the Roman empire, the labour of an industrious and ingenious people was variously, but incessantly employed, in the service of the rich. In their dress, their table, their houses, and their furniture, the favourites of fortune united every refinement of conveniency, of elegance, and of splendor, whatever could soothe their pride or gratify their sensuality. Such refinements, under the odious name of luxury, have been severely arraigned by the moralists of every age; and it might perhaps be more conducive to the virtue, as well as happiness, of mankind, if all possessed the necessaries, and none the superfluities, of life. But in the present imperfect condition of society, luxury, though it may proceed from vice or folly, seems to be the only means that can correct the unequal distribution of property. (I:48)

In fact, luxury did not solve anything, not because it was inefficient in wealth generation, but because it sapped defensive capability, and because it was unjust. The civility produced by commerce alone proved to be quite vulnerable. Luxury produced resentment and unrest. There was a shift back to the values of the East ("the immemorial possession of arts and luxury").

Under Constantine, soldiers "contracted only the vices of civil life":

> They were either degraded by the industry of mechanic trades, or enervated by the luxury of baths and theatres. They soon became careless of their martial exercises, curious in their diet and apparel, and, while they inspired terror to the subjects of the empire, they trembled at the hostile approach of the barbarians. (I:539)

Less civilized countries might be militarily much more effective. In his observations on the "manners of pastoral nations," Gibbon noted that "the pastoral manners, which have been adorned with the fairest attributes of peace and innocence, are much better adapted to the fierce and cruel habits of military life" (I:901). The theme returns again and again in Gibbon's narrative:

> In the various states of society, armies are recruited from very different motives. Barbarians are urged by their love of war; the citizens of a free republic may be prompted by a principle of duty; the subjects, or at least the nobles, of a monarchy are animated by a sentiment of honour; but the timid and luxurious inhabitants of a declining empire must be allured into the service by the hopes of profit, or compelled by the dread of punishment. (I:541)

Gibbon had no doubt that this was an inefficient way of organizing defense. There was no need for him to make the obvious point of the North American dependence of King George III on the ineffective services of paid Hessian mercenaries. In his memoirs, he narrates his own experience as a captain of the Hampshire militia.[15]

Rome and civilization contrast with the barbarian countries because of the disparities of incomes that increased with the development of civilization:

> In a civilised state, every faculty of man is expanded and exercised; and the great mutual chain of dependence connects and embraces the several

members of society. The most numerous portion of it is employed in constant and useful labour. The select few, placed by fortune above that necessity, can, however, fill up their time by the pursuits of interest or glory, by the improvement of their estate or of their understanding, by the duties, the pleasures, and even the follies of social life. The Germans were not possessed of their varied resources. (I:193)

The Roman vision lost its intellectual dynamism at the same time as its capacity for defense eroded, for the same reasons: social emulation. Popularization cheapened and weakened ideas. Hedonism and consumption eroded the social fabric by undermining values.

The authority of Plato and Aristotle, of Zeno and Epicurus, still reigned in the schools; and their systems, transmitted with blind deference from one generation of disciples to another, precluded every generous attempt to exercise the powers, or enlarge the limits, of the human mind. . . . A cloud of critics, of compilers, of commentators, darkened the face of learning, and the decline of genius was soon followed by the corruption of taste. (I:51–52)

In response to the evidence of decline, there were, of course, periodic attempts to restore the ancient rule of virtue. Decius tried to restore the old office of Censor. "He soon discovered that it was impossible to replace that greatness on a permanent basis without restoring public virtue, ancient principles and manners, and the oppressed majesty of the laws." War frustrated this ambition. "The approaching event of war soon put an end to the prosecution of a project so specious but so impracticable" (I:216–17). Rome was in an impossible bind. There was a need to reform morals in order to produce a really sturdy army, but the immediate necessities of organizing for war precluded any thorough remaking and recasting of society.

The cost of defense mounted. Marcus Aurelius, who together with Julian was Gibbon's ideal of a Roman emperor, wanted to restore the peaceful empire of Augustus.

War he detested, as the disgrace and calamity of human nature; but when the necessity of a just defence called upon him to take arms, he readily exposed his person to eight winter campaigns on the frozen banks of the Danube, the severity of which was at last fatal to the weakness of his constitution. (I:69)

Decay thus became unavoidable:

> From the reign of Augustus to the time of Alexander Severus, the enemies of
> Rome were in her bosom; the tyrants and the soldiers; and her prosperity
> had a very distant and feeble interest in the revolutions that might happen
> beyond the Rhine and the Euphrates. But when the military order had lev-
> elled, in wild anarchy, the power of the prince, the laws of the senate, and
> even the discipline of the camp, the barbarians of the North and of the East,
> who had long hovered on the frontier, boldly attacked the provinces of a de-
> clining monarchy. (I:169)

The empire thus faced constant and corrosive distant wars on the
periphery:

> The Romans, who so coolly and so concisely mention the acts of *justice*
> which were exercised by their legions, reserved their compassion and their
> eloquence for their own sufferings when the provinces were invaded and
> desolated by the arms of the successful barbarians. The simple circumstan-
> tial narrative (did such a narrative exist) of the ruin of a single town, or the
> misfortunes of a single family, might exhibit an interesting and instructive
> picture of human manners; but the tedious repetition of vague and declara-
> tory complaints would fatigue the attention of the most patient reader.
> (I:940–41)

In a permanent dynamic, reform efforts were confounded by the
legacy of luxury. The emperor Claudius reflected on the disorders of
the state: that

> a people ruined by oppression, and indolent from despair, could no longer
> supply a numerous army with the means of luxury, or even of subsistence;
> that the danger of each individual had increased with the despotism of the
> military order, since princes who tremble on the throne will guard their
> safety by the instant sacrifice of every obnoxious subject. (I:249)

There was also internal dissolution, again produced by the move to
commercial society and to luxury. "Most of the crimes which disturb
the internal peace of society are produced by the restraints which the
necessary, but unequal, laws of property have imposed on the appetites
of mankind, by confining to a few the possession of those objects that
are coveted by the many" (I:75).

Imperial rule became more oppressive, and there was no escape. At the same time, the memory of past liberty made present servitude more painful. Extensive conquests "rendered their conditions more completely wretched than that of the victims of tyranny in any other age or country" (I:71). Modern Europe was less tyrannical because of a division into many states.

The most important revolt against the values of imperial Rome was that of the Christian faith. The rise of Christianity was born on a tide of revulsion against luxury (I:413). Gibbon's chapters dealing with rise of Christianity and the undermining of Roman values became instantly the most famous and contested of the book. From the point of view of Rome, Christianity was corrosive. It was not simply anticlerical prejudice that led Gibbon to identify Constantine, whose conversion shook the old values, as a deeply problematical emperor. Julian the Apostate (who tried to restore paganism) was, on the other hand, one of the great heroes of Gibbon's saga. The argument about Christianity is actually deeply interwoven with the discussion of the weakness of commercial society.

In particular, Christians rejected the Mandevillian maxim that any pleasurable activity for the individual was good for society. "Very different was the reasoning of our devout predecessors; vainly aspiring to imitate the perfection of angels, they disdained, or they affected to disdain, every earthly and corporeal delight. . . . The first sensation of pleasure was marked as the first moment of their abuse. The unfeeling candidate for heaven was instructed, not only to resist the grosser allurements of taste or smell but even to shut his ears against the profane harmony of sounds, and to view with indifference the most finished productions of human art" (I:413). The Christians turned against commerce.

"The Christians," Gibbon concluded, "were not less adverse to the business than to the pleasures of this world." But then the love of action, though not the love of business revived: "The primitive Christians were dead to the business and pleasures of the world; but their love of action, which could never be entirely extinguished, soon revived, and found a new occupation in the government of the church" (I:416–17). The revolt against luxury thus ended with the establishment of an unproductive and censorious bureaucracy.

When Gibbon tried to present a general summary, at the end of the third quarto volume of the *Decline and Fall*, in "General Observations on the Fall of the Roman Empire in the West," he disappointed almost every modern analyst, because he seems to deny that there is a really interesting story. "The decline of Rome was the natural and inevitable result of immoderate greatness." This conclusion seemed so much less subtle than the long stream of historical analysis, and Gibbon began to sound apologetic about its banality: "The story of its ruin is simple and obvious; and instead of inquiring *why* the Roman empire was destroyed, we should rather be surprised that it had subsisted so long" (II:438). There was something that made Gibbon draw back from presenting too explicit a comparison with the present.

John Pocock sees Gibbon as steeped in the tradition of a Machiavellian civic humanism with a powerful ideal of virtue as found in political association with a republican form. Yet Gibbon's grand story is on the cusp of a turning to a romantic pessimism associated more with Jean-Jacques Rousseau: a recognition of a "Paradox that what makes society move away from savagery and toward virtue and civilization simultaneously undermines its foundations with corruption, so that even virtue and freedom never quite coincide—the latter tending toward savagery, the former toward corruption."[16] Pocock also states that while this idea seems to permeate the structure of Gibbon's argument, it is never quite formulated as a general lesson on the story of the fall of Roman civilization.

Actually, Gibbon did not really need to formulate the conclusion very directly. His readers could easily be expected to reach it through their own devices. Indeed they did.

The analysis of political corruption looked familiar. There is a heavy irony about the life of the master of eighteenth-century irony. He wrote his indictment of corruption as a source of decay, comfortably funded as a placeman and sinecure holder of Lord North. This dependence excited some satire. Someone, possibly the great oppositionalist and parliamentary orator Charles James Fox, wrote verses that are usually supposed to have been found in Fox's copy of *Decline and Fall*:

His book well describes
How corruption and bribes

CHAPTER ONE

O'erthrew the great empire of Rome;
And his writings declare
A degen'racy there
Which his conduct exhibits at home.[17]

There are many points of overlap between the work of Smith and Gibbon. Perhaps this is not surprising, for they were friends and maintained some sort of correspondence. They were also responding to the peculiarities of a specific historical moment. Their books are really parallel parables of a commercial rise and fall.

Like Gibbon, Smith starts in the *Wealth of Nations* with an examination of commercial prosperity. This is undoubtedly the best known and remembered part of the work. The famous account of the pin factory as an example of the productivity-enhancing effect of division of labor occurs within a page of the opening of the book. Some modern readers and most modern popularizers of Smith are so happy with the account presented in Book I that they never seem to get beyond this, and it is this section of the book that gave rise to the caricature that is preserved in nineteenth-century versions of "Smithianismus." It is also striking how the celebrations of both the centenary and the bicentenary of the *Wealth of Nations* rested on the assumption that the world of Smith, and that the world of the present, was fundamentally peaceful. On May 31, 1876, the Political Economy Club held a dinner at which William Gladstone took the chair, and the keynote speaker, Robert Lowe explained that Smith had failed only "because he had not sufficient confidence in the truth of the doctrines which he laid down."[18] In 1976, the mood was much less enthusiastic about the possibilities of the market, and at the major celebration of the book, Alec Cairncross thought that Smith had underplayed the role that the state could and should play: "It was the shortcomings of the state in its efforts to encourage development and improvement that disposed him to scepticism of its pretensions. No doubt he overstated the case."[19] Both the market and the state made for peace, according to the celebratory speakers. Actually, as should have been obvious to Smith's readers, the pin factory is just the beginning: it has a role that is analogous to the story of the Garden of Eden at the commencement of the biblical narrative.

Most readers of Smith seem to have stopped before they reach Book V.

This last section of the *Wealth of Nations* is devoted to the examination of the Roman predicament. Parts read like an abbreviated version of *Decline and Fall*. Smith shares all of Gibbon's distaste for academics and monks. "In the university of Oxford," Smith says, "the greater part of the public professors have, for these many years, given up altogether even the pretense of teaching."[20] The clergy usually represent a drain on society. Gibbon in Oxford as a student had suffered first hand from the "monks at Magdalen."[21] Why should intellectuals and especially the clergy be so parasitical and pernicious? The argument depends on a complex and sophisticated account of the political economy of commercial development.

First of all, there was a general reason why commercial states might be vulnerable. Wealth inevitably excites envy, and thus produces a security problem.

> The wealth, at the same time, which always follows the improvements of agriculture and manufactures, and which in reality is no more than the accumulated produce of those improvements, provokes the invasion of all their neighbours. An industrious, and upon that account a wealthy nation, is of all nations the most likely to be attacked; and unless the state takes some new measures for the public defence, the natural habits of the people render them altogether incapable of defending themselves. (II:220)

The story of the Netherlands in the seventeenth century offered a grim precedent of a state that was commercially successful but was forced to defend itself in wars that proved ruinously costly.[22]

Like every writer on politics at this time, Smith saw defense as the "first duty of the sovereign." The burden was not inevitably very costly for a state of a certain size, because Smith knew that he was living in an age of high tech and increasingly one-sided warfare. Advanced states have an advantage in that they can use technology for their defense. "The art of war, however, as it is certainly the noblest of all the arts, so in the progress of improvement becomes one of the most complicated among them" (II:219). Civilization, as Smith saw it, therefore depended on gun powder.

> In modern war the great expense of fire-arms gives an evident advantage to the nation which can best afford that expence; and consequently, to an

opulent and civilized, over a poor and barbarous nation . . . In modern times the poor and barbarous find it difficult to defend themselves against the opulent and civilized. The invention of firearms, an invention which at first sight appears to be so pernicious, is certainly favourable both to the permanency and to the extension of civilization. (II:230–31)

Technical superiority may thus give a commercial state a substantial measure of strength. Commerce does not necessarily mean Dutch-style vulnerability. Smith saw another sort of problem at the center of the need for defense. He was worried about the effect of the projection of power and of armies on social disparities. He saw a debate about who benefited from arms and empire.

Book V of *Wealth of Nations* thus contains an extensive account of the relative merits of militias and standing armies. As war becomes more technical, it requires greater expertise. The principle of the division of labor so dramatically enunciated right at the start of Book I clearly applies here as elsewhere, which, Smith thought, made it advisable to have a military class. "The division of labor is as necessary for the improvement of this, as of every other art" (II:219).

There might, however, be high political costs of a standing army. In particular, the historical example of the end of the Roman Republic was a sober warning. It had been destroyed by Caesar's standing army; but "where the sovereign is himself the general," a standing army might in some cases be favorable to liberty (II:229). On the other hand, a militia that fights several successive campaigns might become as professional as a standing army. Smith thought that he could see this process of increased competence in the course of the American Revolutionary War, as George Washington managed to produce an effective fighting force out of initially highly local, centrifugal, and quarrelsome militias. A militia avoided the political costs of the standing army.

The same rationale that requires advanced ("civilized") states to protect themselves against external enemies also requires a defense against internal threats of disorder. Again there existed a threat to political order and stability, which Smith saw as a vivid reality in eighteenth-century Britain.

Smith worried more than most of his later apologists about distributional issues. Advanced states are also unequal states. In them, the rich are only rich because of the protection of law.

But avarice and ambition in the rich, in the poor the hatred of labour and the love of present ease and enjoyment, are the passions which prompt to invade property, passions much more steady in their operation, and much more universal in their influence. Wherever there is great property, there is great inequality. For one very rich man, there must be at least five hundred poor, and the affluence of the few supposes the indigence of the many. The affluence of the rich excites the indignation of the poor, who are often both driven by want, and prompted by envy, to invade his possessions. It is only under the shelter of the civil magistrate that the owner of that valuable property, which is acquired by the labour of many years, or perhaps of many successive generations, can sleep a single night in security. (II:232)

Such a diminution of wealth and resources created constant vulnerability, and required for enhanced protection the extension of political power. This was in Smith's view hardly a healthy development.

The division of labor might be deadening to the moral and intellectual imagination. Again, Smith offers in Book V the converse of the happy picture that he presented at the outset of Book I. The effect of the division of labor in confining working men and women to "a few simple operations" is deeply destructive. The workman

naturally loses, therefore, the habit of such exertion, and generally becomes as stupid and ignorant as it is possible for a human creature to become. The torpor of his mind renders him, not only incapable of relishing or bearing a part in any rational conversation, but of conceiving any generous, noble, or tender sentiment, and consequently of forming any just judgment concerning many even of the ordinary duties of private life.

By contrast, in "barbarous societies," "Invention is kept alive, and the mind is not suffered to fall into that drowsy stupidity, which, in a civilized society, seems to benumb the understanding of almost all the inferior ranks of people" (II:303).

In his earlier work, *The Theory of the Moral Sentiments*, Smith had offered a sort of trickle-down version of why the poor might find commercial but unequal society acceptable. "The rich . . . consume little more than the poor. . . . They are led by an invisible hand to make nearly the same distribution of the necessaries of life which would have been made had the earth been divided into equal portions among all its inhabitants."[23] In the *Wealth of Nations*, there is no analogous passage.

Instead, in the *Wealth of Nations*, the section on the stultification produced by the division of labor is followed immediately by Smith's major treatment of religion. Religion offers the poor the possibility of escape from immorality and meaninglessness. When the workman

> comes into a great city, he is sunk in obscurity and darkness. His conduct is observed and attended to by nobody, and he is therefore very likely to neglect it himself, and to abandon himself to every sort of low profligacy and vice. He never emerges so effectually from this obscurity, his conduct never excites so much the attention of any respectable society, as by his becoming the member of a small religious sect. (II:317)

This was essentially the story that Gibbon told about the emergence of Christianity in the Roman Empire.

Smith thus devoted a great deal of his attention in the later stages of his argument to the way in which the public interest could be subverted by accumulations of vast and unaccountable wealth. In particular he attacked the idea of joint stock companies, and the implicit separation of ownership from management:

> The directors of such companies, however, being the managers rather of other people's money than of their own, it cannot well be expected, that they should watch over it with the same anxious vigilance with which the partners in a private copartnery frequently watch over their own. Like the stewards of a rich man, they are apt to consider attention to small matters as not for their master's honour, and very easily give themselves a dispensation from having it. Negligence and profusion, therefore, must always prevail, more or less, in the management of the affairs of such a company. (II:264–65)

Such companies, in particular the East India Company and the African Company, had distorted foreign policy for the sake of procuring private gains. As the East India Company became richer, its officials became ever more corrupt. "The great increase of their fortune had, it seems, only served to furnish their servants with a pretext for greater profusion, and a cover for greater malversation, than in proportion even to that increase in fortune" (II:274). Unlike real governments, these companies could not be controlled, and they had no incentive at all to behave with restraint or responsibility.

> No other sovereigns ever were, or, from the nature of things, ever could be, so perfectly indifferent about the happiness or misery of their subjects, the improvement or waste of their dominions, the glory or disgrace of their administration; as, from irresistible moral causes, the greater part of the proprietors of such a mercantile company are, and necessarily must be. (II:276)

Smith ended his observations with a calculation of the financial gains and losses of empire: a devastating balance sheet that leaves little doubt that Britain, far from being at the height of an imperial prosperity, was running substantial risks. The calculation comes after a long examination of the high levels of public debt in Britain and the consequent difficulty in fighting expensive colonial wars. He ends the book with a damning indictment of British policy:

> The rulers of Great Britain have, for more than a century past, amused the people with the imagination that they possessed a great empire on the west side of the Atlantic. This empire, however, has hitherto existed in imagination only. It has hitherto been, not an empire, but the project of an empire; not a gold mine, but the project of a gold mine; a project which has cost, which continues to cost, and which, if pursued in the same way as it has been hitherto, is likely to cost, immense expence, without being likely to bring any profit.

The final words of Smith's great book are an injunction to free Britain from the expense of war and "endeavour to accommodate her future views and designs to the real mediocrity of her circumstances" (II:486).

One important feature of the Roman story stood out for both Gibbon and Smith. Rome was so compelling a case, not just because it was a great commercial and imperial power and because it had declined, but also because the decline was connected in some way with the development of the major religion of modern European civilization. A century or so after Smith and Gibbon, Feodor Dostoevsky made the point in a horrifically striking way when he speculated in *Notes from the Underground* about a world of great prosperity in which there would be "nothing else to do but sleep, eat cakes, and only worry about keeping world history going."[24] Ancient Rome was also a world of almost unimaginable cruelty, in which Cleopatra had stuck her golden needles into the breasts of slave girls; and it was the world in which Christ had appeared. Rome looked like the model for commercial society in both its virtues and its vices. It was a symbol of massive power, but at the same time of a challenge that it could not meet.

The Roman Empire assimilated new areas into its imperial rule by incorporating the local theologies into a pluralistic religious universe. More gods could simply be added to the capacious Roman pantheon, and local deities would sit alongside the imperial gods without rivalry or clashes. Polytheism was based on a deep but politically motivated respect for difference and local tradition. Romans saw polytheism as a basis for imperial rule, so that Rome became the center of world religions: not just of the worship of the classic Roman gods, but also of the cults of Mithras, or Egyptian celebrations, and, of course, the highly intolerant Christianity.

The twenty-first-century equivalent, in a world in which the central culture is no longer religious, is multiculturalism: the encouragement of a broad diversity of cultures with a call for mutual tolerance and comprehension. Inhabitants of industrial countries are proud that they no longer just have "Western" music or traditional cuisine; they patronize oriental incense and mysticisms as well as scent-shops with French perfumes. The result has without doubt made modern life, particularly modern urban existence, much more interesting and rewarding.

Yet it involves the suspension of a particular human facility, that of judgment. Diversity means the enthusiastic acceptance of other practices, and a restraint on judgment about difference or "the other." "Judgmental" becomes a damning attribute. The only basis for decision-making becomes a contentless utilitarianism, an approach originally developed at the moment when Europe was beginning its universal embrace. Jeremy Bentham famously argued that from the perspective of the legislator, it was important that pushpins were as valuable as poetry.

In the following chapters, the argument will be set out that integration across large geographic and cultural distances requires well-understood and well-applied rules if it is not to be seen as capricious and arbitrary. If this is true, then the drive to polytheism or its modern analogue of multiculturalism poses a major problem. The stage is then set for another "Roman predicament": either there is disintegration because of a proliferation of values, or disintegration because the imposition by force of one set of values provokes an inexorable and violent backlash. The Roman Empire recast itself under Constantine—in the move that Gibbon so deplored—from polytheism to monotheism. The subsequent attempts at universal or world rule (or an approximation of it)—of the Christianized Roman Empire, or of the early phase of Islamic expansion, linked world domination with a single set of values, or monotheism.[25] But the combination of monotheism or a strong version of a single and coherently defined set of beliefs, coming from the non-Western world, is likely to provoke continual contestation and clashes. The frontier will become unsettled, and the center corrupted.

Mercury and Mars

At the beginning of the twenty-first century, the world of Adam Smith and Edward Gibbon may seem very remote, but their answers to the questions raised by the process of globalization remain astonishingly acute. Is there a single dominant world power, and what are its limits and weaknesses? Is there a single set of values, a modern equivalent of the Roman shift to monotheism, that is imposed as part of a new imperialism?

The process of economic convergence that in the last years of the twentieth century produced the widening of the "West" into a universal concept was facilitated by the movement across national frontiers of goods, capital, labor, ideas, and technologies. In short it came about as a result of the phenomenon now widely referred to as "globalization." This is a much older process than is suggested by the history of the term, which really only began to appear in widespread use during the early 1980s. This chapter examines the conceptual foundation of "globalization."

Globalization is not a continuous process. In periods when obstacles to the movement of economic factors (and also ideas) were raised—above all in the interwar period of the twentieth century—the process of convergence was halted and reversed. Convergence resumed for the Cold War "West" after 1948–49, and then—after the political and economic upheavals of 1989–91—more or less universally. By the 1990s, as Russia, India, Mexico, and Korea, with quite different trajectories for most of the past century and with strong traditions of nationalist economic management, all became, in an economic sense, "Western." They accepted a mix of commitments: to the rule of law, to democracy as a way of setting rules, and to free interchange (the market) as a way of optimizing outcomes within a secure system of property rights.

By the end of the twentieth century, the world had become "Western," although there was a great deal of ambiguity about the meaning of the term. Was it a reference to U.S. values, or to a U.S.–European mixture, or did it refer to advanced industrial countries—Japan, Europe, and the United States—whose policies were discussed and sometimes even coordinated at Group of Seven meetings? The new climate was neatly described in a famous exchange at a meeting on a U.S. battleship off the coast of Malta in December 1989, which is often held to mark the end of the Cold War. When U.S. Secretary of State James Baker talked about the need to make a possibly reunified Germany more secure through the cementation of "Western values," Mikhail Gorbachev, the general secretary of the Communist Party of the Soviet Union, asked why democracy and the market were "Western" and whether they were not values which "belonged to the whole of humanity"?[26] The world established by freedom (in other words, political choice and choice in the market as parallel processes) continues to have a powerful appeal. Above all, it seems to guarantee peace. Is it, however, so appealing that it persuades everyone and that everyone is consequently pacific? There must be some doubts on that score.

However bad security relations are between what can now really be called the opposed sides of the Atlantic, or whatever spats there are across the Pacific on the value of the renminbi and the yen, there is a frequent hope that the strength and complexity of the economic interrelationship (a product of globalization) is so great as to offer a counterweight to the political tensions. Indeed the reason that both sides in modern conflicts feel that they can afford to be rhetorically carried away is a function of the sense of interdependence, and that a really bad outcome is not possible. The British Prime Minister Harold Macmillan, for instance, liked to tell President Kennedy that a "united Free World was more likely to be achieved through joint monetary and economic policies" than through political or military alliances.[27] Advanced democracies do not go to war with each other, as they have too much to lose.[28] Mercury, the god of commerce, has managed to send Mars, the god of war, into exile. We feel very secure about this argument and its implications—maybe we feel too secure.

There are periods in the past when greatly increasing prosperity attracted many commentators to similar arguments: in the mid-nineteenth century, before the Crimean war, or in the early twentieth century. In John Henry Newman's *Apologia pro vita sua* (1864), for instance, Newman uses the widely asserted association between commerce and peace, familiar from the works of the great British apostles of free trade, Richard Cobden and John Bright, to reach a verdict on attempts at

> expedients to arrest fierce wilful human nature in its onward course, and bring it into subjection: ten years ago there was a hope that wars would cease for ever, under the influence of commercial enterprise and the reign of the useful and fine arts; but will anyone venture to say that there is any thing any where on this earth, which will afford a fulcrum to us, whereby to keep the earth from moving onwards?[29]

The most famous or notorious account of the idea that there was a "fact" of the modern world, namely that "intangible economic forces are setting at nought the force of arms" came in Norman Angell's *The Great Illusion* (1909). Angell's work was aimed at showing how the character of rule and empire had changed as a consequence of economic interdependence. He saw in this a fundamental contrast to imperialism of the Roman model, which relied on the extraction of tribute from subject populations:

> Rome did not have to create markets and to find a field for the employment of her capital. We do. What result does this carry? Rome could afford to be relatively indifferent to the prosperity of her subject territory. We cannot. If the territory is not prosperous we have no market, and we have no field for our investments, and that is why we are checked at every point from doing what Rome was able to do.[30]

Supposing, however, that there existed for the governing elite an irresistible urge to behave like Rome. Then Bright and Cobden and Angell might be wrong, and Newman would be right.

What was the origin of the fallacy Newman detected? If it were true that economics determines the way political and security relations work, there would evidently be harmony between the major industrial countries. We would slide into a sort of Fukuyama *post-histoire*, a vision elaborated with power and clarity after 1989. This harmony is frequently evoked in the "globalization paradigm." Many people, particularly those involved with business, repeatedly emphasize that the world is closely connected, and that political boundaries and arguments are irrelevant to business logic. For all the political friction since September 11 and the Iraq war, there have been increased flows of funds and investments, and the extent of economic connectivity has become greater rather than less. Many people who think of themselves as living in a globalization mindset would like to operationalize this economic interconnectedness, and make the fact of interdependent prosperity a building stone for better international relations.

They can do this because of the idea that rules are at the basis of policy interactions that make globalization possible. The easiest way to understand this is in terms of a debate, which is sometimes just confined to economists, of the virtues of rules versus discretion. Modern writers tend to shift in favor of rules rather than discretion, and elaborate models of behavior in which binding oneself by rules produces better outcomes. In the most famous example of this, which has had widespread influence on central bank design, countries will do better by tying themselves to a monetary regime managed by a politically independent central bank with a rule that prevents the inflationary management of the currency. Otherwise observers will notice that unexpected bursts of inflation can raise production and hence also employment (with a politically positive effect), largely because they lead to reduced real wages, while if inflation is expected the stimulatory effects will be countered by wage increases. If wage negotiators see a government in a politically sensitive situation, for instance when building a coalition or facing an election, they may expect an inflationary surge and wages will rise. If the government actually does push inflation, the effect on output and employment will thus be neutralized, and if the government exercises self-restraint, the effect will be negative. The results are thus better if the government ostentatiously ties its hands, and wage-setters realize that there is nothing the government can do.

Such results apply to other policy areas as well, as in the management of financial crises. An awareness that there is a public authority capable of stepping in with a bailout or rescue may encourage reckless behavior by depositors, investors, and bankers: thus in the U.S. savings and loans crisis of the 1980s, deposit insurance made depositors unconcerned about their banks, so that they stopped monitoring the behavior and reputation of the banks, which then embarked on highly risky investment strategies. Where there is no possibility of a rescue, there may be less lending, but there is also less bad risk that is pushed onto public authority.

The application of such ideas does not stop with monetary and financial regulation. Arms limitation or reduction agreements, and provisions for the inspection of weapons and armament-producing facilities can create confidence by ruling out an inflationary approach to weapons procurement. As in the case of monetary inflation, negotiated rules stop a vicious circle, in which states behave like cats chasing their own tails. This is why any vision of the world as an interactive whole— that is, "globalization"—requires a system of rules.

Is globalization the only show in town? The major alternative to the "globalization" worldview sees connectedness as producing unfair advantages, and international relations as based on exploitation. One convenient way of labeling this alternative is "imperialism," a word generally used with a critical intent. Labeling U.S. policy as "imperialism" became part of the standard rhetorical weaponry of an anti-American left in Europe and elsewhere, as well as of critical voices in the United States. The school of diplomatic history under William Appleman Williams strongly engaged in this approach.[31] In the 1990s, the language of empire as a way of critiquing power, and especially American power, was revived—most influentially by the Italian philosopher of violent revolution from the 1970s, Toni Negri, who now became a guru for the anti-globalization left. After September 11, 2001, and especially after the Iraq war, this worldview produced a tremendous spate of books.[32]

In particular, the Roman analogy, which had already been floated just before and after World War II in response to Roosevelt's bold initiatives for a new level of American engagement in the international order, became very popular: critics saw the imperialization of the United States as an analogous process to the ending of the Roman Republic and its replacement by the Augustan empire. The passionately critical American historian Charles Beard in the late 1930s feared Roosevelt's engagement in European issues, which he castigated as a continuation of the "frenzy for foreign adventurism." He derided Walter Lippmann's appeal that "what Rome was to the ancient world, what Great Britain has been to the modern world, America is to be to the world of tomorrow." According to Beard, by contrast, "Rome conquered, ruled, and robbed other peoples from the frontier in Scotland to the sands of Arabia, from the Rhine to the Sahara, and then crumbled to ruins. Does anybody in his right mind really believe that the United States can or ought to play that role in the future, or anything akin to it?" Beard traced the distortion of American foreign policy to the prophet of sea power Alfred Thayer Mahan, whose imagination had been captured by Theodor Mommsen's history of Rome. By the late 1990s, in the aftermath of the Cold War, and as American outreach expanded, this kind of critique appealed once more.[33]

Curiously, however, this mostly critical literature began to be supplemented by normative suggestions that the United States should want to behave like an empire of the European past. At the conclusion of a stimulating survey of the story of the British empire, Niall Ferguson tried to draw "lessons for global power." The United States, he concluded, first of all "can do a great deal to impose its preferred values on less technologically advanced societies."[34] The suggestion was that it would be drawn in through a series of interventions analogous to those of nineteenth-century Britain, and would create a functioning imperial system without really willing or knowing it. (One famous phrase, coined by the great British historian J. R. Seeley, claims that the Victorian empire was put together in a fit of absence of mind). Michael Ignatieff, reflecting on the legacies of Bosnia and Rwanda, added an appeal for a dynamic human rights internationalism, which he termed "Empire Lite."[35]

Most figures associated with the U.S. administration even in the Bush presidency did not like the idea of taking up Caesar's mantle or Victoria's tiara. Yet Vice President and Lynne Cheney in 2003 sent out a Christmas card with a quotation from Benjamin Franklin: "And if a sparrow cannot fall to the ground without His notice, is it probable that an empire can rise without His aid?"[36]

The new discussion of imperialism as a model is quite perplexing. In particular, some committed institutional liberal internationalists such as John Ikenberry have pointed out that Empire Lite actually looks like old-fashioned liberal internationalism.[37] What is new? The story of some of the human rights catastrophes of the 1990s, notably in Rwanda and Bosnia, as well as the novel nature of the challenge of international terrorism, raise the obvious issue that there are many people who will go to considerable lengths and make suicidal sacrifices to undermine a liberal and tolerant international and national order. How, in the absence of a world government, can they be kept in line? Only by the application of force by the hegemon.

Many readers will feel that it is possible to see both the world views presented here at the same time: that in the spirit of Empire Lite, rules without enforcement are bound to be ignored, and enforcement without fixed rules is likely to be widely rejected as arbitrary or tyrannical. Therefore both rules and an enforcer (who is a state) are needed for stability and order. There is a well-established literature, based on the work of Charles Kindleberger and Robert Gilpin, which suggests that the nineteenth-century liberal order worked only because of the benign hegemon and that after 1945 the United States learned this lesson.[38] This is known in the academic literature as the "hegemonic stability" thesis.

As an interpretation of the nineteenth century, "hegemonic stability" never looked very convincing. In economics, the case looks very dubious. Britain dominated some of the classic industries of the industrial revolution, and continued to be a major exporter of coal and cotton textiles. Most contemporaries, as well as subsequent analysts, have taken steel production as the key indicator of an economic good that could be translated directly into power, since steel meant ships and guns. But in steel, Britain was outproduced by the end of the nineteenth century by Germany and the United States. In fact, Britain could never act as a power hegemon in respect either to continental Europe or to the United States, and continental Europeans thought of power relations in terms of a Great Game played by a substantial number of players (five, or perhaps even seven). Britain's empire amounted to alliances with increasingly autonomous white settler colonies, the control of India, a leading part in the division of Africa, and the maintenance of a large number of naval bases giving an impressive sea power reach across the world.

This was a very different situation compared to the post-1945 world, which really did correspond for a few decades to the theory of "hegemonic stability." U.S. economic power was practically unchallenged: in

1945, the United States accounted for an amazing half of the world's production of manufactured goods. The statistic actually understates the extent of U.S. preeminence, in that with the defeat of Germany the United States was the only significant producer of machine tools, in other words, of the complex equipment needed by other countries if they were to follow the path of industrialization. It was consequently easy for U.S. policymakers to see that they could use economic power as an obvious weapon of security policy, and to bind Western Europe and Japan to the United States by economic ties. It was also relatively easy for them to persuade the American political process that such a use of economic tools was in the interests of the American people and the American economy. Without a general prosperity, there would be no market for U.S. goods, and there would be a risk of the repetition of the economic disasters of the interwar era. The most obvious embodiment of the new U.S. approach was the Marshall Plan for the economic recovery of Europe, sketched out by Secretary of State George Marshall in a series of speeches at major American universities between February and June 1947.

Kindleberger, one of the major architects of the "hegemonic stability" theory, was involved in the implementation of the Marshall Plan. It is not surprising that the theory looks like a generalization of the plan. This generation of planners and economists also took a rather different approach to the rules-versus-discretion debate from that taken by more recent analysts. In their view, the catastrophe and misery of the interwar years had been the result of the over-rigid following of bad monetary rules, and of the restrictive philosophy that "There Is No Alternative" (a view dubbed as "TINA" when enunciated by Margaret Thatcher in the early 1980s). Even in the 1990s, Kindleberger still defended his view that crisis solution depended on the ability of brilliant men to devise innovative and novel solutions, and that the pedantic following of rules was unwise and counterproductive. "With strong and cohesive leadership, near unanimity of experts and understanding or pliant followership, men can be trusted to perform better than rules." This was the Marshall Plan scenario, but—as Kindleberger implies—it rests on the use of political power to override the rules, the phenomenon that Kindleberger labels, perhaps euphemistically, as "strong and cohesive leadership."[39]

31

The idea that the world's problems can be solved by a new Marshall Plan orchestrated by a benevolent hegemon has been perennially attractive at moments of crisis and transformation. After the collapse of the Soviet empire in central Europe, and then again after the collapse of the Soviet Union itself, a flood of articles and policy speeches and academic books called for a revived Marshall Plan. The same point has been made in regard to the Middle East: namely that reconstruction after war and catastrophe cannot occur without some external impetus or jump start.

Such plans for reviving the ghost of George Marshall in new circumstances were not realized. Retrospectively, the uniqueness of the post-1945 moment becomes ever more apparent. The same calculation that appeared so obvious in 1947–48 would in subsequent decades require a much more complex and costly trade-off. It would no longer be a case of the hegemon spending abroad to assure markets and preeminence and thus building its power in an effectively costless way. Rather, big transfers would clearly nurture new powers and new rivals, and the German and Japanese economies emerged as powerful and scary competitors to the United States. It was easy to point out that defeated and largely demilitarized Germany and Japan had a great advantage, in that they allocated less public spending to costly military objectives, as they benefited from a strategic U.S. guarantee. In consequence, a great deal of the literature began to focus on the exhaustion or "weariness" of the hegemon. "For internal and external reasons," Gilpin concluded, "the hegemonic power loses both its will and its ability to manage the system."[40] Some commentators consequently used the theory to forecast the necessary decline of the hegemon.

Why did the system nevertheless remain in place for so long? The post-1945 calculation and the Marshall Plan model could last as they did because of the Cold War and the consequent bipolarity of international relations. The economic choices were locked in place by a military threat. It was not so much U.S. power or military presence but the threat of Soviet power that gave the United States such a major position in European and Asian politics. (Correspondingly, the Soviet Union tried to instrumentalize a threat of U.S. and imperialist encirclement to justify its imposition of power on its sphere of influence in central Europe. Stalin's encirclement speech in the Bolshoi theater on

February 9, 1946, marked the beginning of the hardening of the Soviet approach.)

The uniquely successful U.S. role in reconstructing Western Europe also depended on an ethical rationale, and not simply on nuclear weapons and massive land forces. The Cold War provoked a thinking about values. The economic choices were worked into a larger theory of a community of values, a "West," that needed an intellectual as well as a military and an economic defense. The new view of Europe was built up by journals such as Melvin Lasky's *Der Monat* in Germany, Ignazio Silone's *Tempo presente* in Italy, and *Encounter* in London, sponsored by the Congress for Cultural Freedom and indirectly by the U.S. Central Intelligence Agency. The new Europeanism reflected a hard line on foreign policy issues combined with social democratic reformism in domestic issues. As seen by the proponents of the idea of the Western community, it was not so much hegemony or money that made for the success of the Marshall vision, but a framework of values. Without power or money, however, ideas would have looked feeble, as they had done in the interwar era when democracy and liberalism were criticized as incapable of dealing with the basic economic and social problems of the modern world.

By the last decades of the Cold War, with greater stability in international relations and greater cynicism in domestic politics, the idea of the community of values was beginning to look tired and weary. The idea of a "West" was swept away by 1989: *Encounter*, for instance, ceased publication in September 1990, just a few months after the end of the Cold War. For a few years it looked as if the "globalization" paradigm reigned supreme, with a world held together by rules rather than by power or by values. Yet the advocates of "globalization" always had a problem in thinking about the origins of rules for the new world order.

Generally, the rules approach demands a participation in the formulation of the binding rules of a broad group of countries, views, and interests. Without such participation, the rules began to lack legitimacy (unless it is generally agreed that the rules stem from a divinely created natural law order, but this, perhaps unfortunately, does not seem an attractive proposition to most modern thinkers). The more a generalized relativism guides our approach to rule-making, the more we insist on process as the way of creating legitimacy. These processes, however, are actually deeply divisive in practice, and the most intractable tussles of recent years arise out of arguments about the rule-making process in such institutions as the United Nations, the World Trade Organization, the International Monetary Fund, and the European Union. A tremendous amount of ingenuity is spent on devising organizational and institutional solutions: reforming the Security Council of the United Nations; extending the Group of Seven to encompass Russia in a G-8 and then China; and reshaping the international financial institutions (the so-called "international financial architecture" debate). The logistics of voting arrangements in international and supranational organizations is hotly contested: the weighted votes at the IMF and the World Bank, the difference between permanent members of the Security Council and the rest, or (in the European setting) the different weights given to big, medium-sized, and small countries in the Nice Treaty of 2001 and the proposed revision in the 2004 constitutional treaty.

In each of the much-discussed cases of an alleged need for institutional reform, there is a sort of expectations trap.[41] International rule-making looks more crucial, and so we have greater hopes about what international negotiation can produce. The IMF is seen as the key to preventing financial crisis and contagion, the UN as the guarantor of world peace. Yet the result is a compromise that is disappointing, and so there arises a substantial questioning of the legitimacy of the process.

As a result, when our hopes of rules are disappointed, we react by seeing power in its full *Realpolitik* nakedness. *Realpolitik* overrides rules, or, as a rather old British pun had it, Britannia waives the rules in order to rule the waves.

The "imperialism" and the "globalization" models are overall interpretations of such power for their respective adherents that the other perspective simply disappears. The alternative is rejected as naïve or ideological, as in Robert Kagan's juxtaposition of the Mars and Venus views of Americans and Europeans.[42] As approaches, they are like the optical illusions made famous by Maurits Cornelius Escher, where squares either pop out of a page, or recede, but where the observer cannot be brought to see both phenomena at the same time. There is one perspective—or the other.

Sometimes these views seem to coexist with each other within the confines of a single institution: say, in the complex structure known as the modern state. Defense ministries are likely to be stuffed with "realists," who view power in terms of a zero-sum game, in which one's own gains must correspond to losses of power elsewhere. Finance or foreign ministries are likely to have many globalists, so much so that they sometimes run into the hackneyed criticism that the foreign ministry is the ministry representing foreigners. The inhabitants of these quite different policy worlds surprisingly rarely engage in any debate with the other side. They simply slug it out for relative institutional influence, in a struggle that really is a zero-sum game: one side either wins or loses.

The way in which the prevailing paradigm shifts from "globalization" to "empire" raises profound questions about how foreign policy should be conducted. At the heart of classical realism is the belief that it is easily possible to determine whether a policy is imperialist or not. Hans Morgenthau's classic exposition in *Politics among Nations* has a short section entitled "How to Detect and Counter an Imperialistic Policy." He explains, "The answer to that question has determined the fate of nations, and the wrong answer has often meant deadly peril or actual destruction; for upon the correctness of that answer depends the success of the foreign policy derived from it."[43] Precision on this is certainly possible in some cases, and Morgenthau was writing in a world still haunted by the experience of Nazi aggression and faced by the reality of Soviet influence and power. But is it always easy to be so sure about an answer to whether policy is imperialistic? Few would want to argue that Luxembourg, at least over the past five centuries, has been an aggressive state, but all states pursue their interests and try to expand their power, and most are accused at some time or other of bending rules and imposing costs on their neighbors. "Imperialism" then becomes an easy slogan to bandy around.

The paradox of realism as an interpretative structure is that the necessary uncertainty about what constitutes aggression and imperialism means that we need to assume that all powers are inherently aggressive or imperialist unless checked by some other power. Only an external code could provide a clear answer to the question of aggression, but realists do not like to see either that there might be such a code or that they really need one. The alternative view has a paradox too, in that the "globalization" mindset knows that it must define rules, but finds it practically hard to make rules that are acceptable.

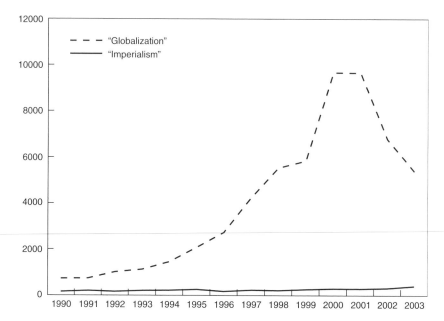

1 Lexis-Nexis citations of "globalization" and "imperialism," 1990–2003

Since 2001, there has been a definite retreat of the "globalization" paradigm. It is evident in a survey of Lexis-Nexis citations of the word "globalization" in major world newspapers, which shows a distinct falling off
after 2001. On the other hand, there are more references to "empire"
and "imperialism." Indeed, "empire" now is quite casually used in a way
that even a few years ago would have been unthinkable. Thus, for instance, the *Financial Times* in late 2004 discussed the international controversy about the disputed presidential election in Ukraine in the following terms: "The EU and Russia, two very different empires, remain
wary of each other—but all too conscious of their mutual dependence."[44] Every large and complex state suddenly seems to be an empire,
and the language of interdependence and globalization has been cast
aside.

Are there any objectively available guides to answer the Morgenthau
question and help us decide whether we should think of ourselves as
living in the rule-based world, or in one that is quite arbitrary? Or is the
choice itself quite arbitrary?

The most obvious guide is the extent to which rules resemble general and universal rules of fairness, and are not particular laws or "privileges." Thus a universally applied tax is legitimate, but not one that applies to particular categories of people: non-aristocrats (as in pre-1789 France, where the aristocracy was largely exempted), or non-Muslims (in the Ottoman Empire), or Jews (in Nazi Germany) to take three of the best-known examples of illiberal regimes. There is also some room for disagreement: to continue with the example of taxation, is a progressive tax, universally applied, fair in that it falls by design more heavily on a particular group of people (the rich); or is a universal consumption tax, evenly applied, fair in that it falls disproportionately heavily on a group of people who consume a higher share of their income (the poor)?

The universality test is the approach taken by traditional liberalism. It achieved its clearest and most distinct twentieth-century interpretation in the work of Friedrich Hayek, above all in *The Constitution of Liberty*. The coercive powers of government must serve general and timeless purposes, and not specific ends.[45] The more every person or object governed by the rule is subject only to a purely Hayekian general determination, the more remote the possibility of discrimination and arbitrariness. Nevertheless there is a problem in this solution, in that states that give their citizens particular privileges by virtue of being citizens thereby subvert the possibility of a pure generality.

Hayek saw this problem very clearly, and in *The Road to Serfdom* concluded,

> It is neither necessary nor desirable that national boundaries should mark sharp differences in standards of living, that membership in a national group should entitle to a share in a cake altogether different from that in which members of other groups share. If the resources of different nations are treated as exclusive properties of these nations as wholes, if international economic relations, instead of being relations between individuals, become increasingly relations between whole nations organised as trading bodies, they inevitably become the source of friction and envy between nations.[46]

In the end, the existence of national states that redistribute income and wealth (and necessarily make different choices about how much of this redistribution they should undertake) is incompatible with the

Hayekian vision. As long as there are separate states making such different choices, they give particular privileges, which will make those excluded focus their resentments on the state units that do the excluding. Only a universal state, with no restrictions on movement, or alternatively national states with no redistribution, could be legitimate. Neither of these options seems remotely plausible or even recognizable in the world as it exists today.

A second approach to the problem of legitimacy is that taken by traditional conservatism: to think that rules are legitimate because they may in origin be quite arbitrary or absurd, but in the course of time they acquire an ever-deeper patina of trust. Legal structures hold generations together over time, according to this interpretation. Since this is a social good and represents the major function of the rule system, we should not press too closely into questions of their original legitimacy. We simply have to take the system as it exists for granted, and we must not question too closely the origins of rules, or of wealth and distribution.

The greatest defect of this conservative approach is not so much that it ignores great historical injustices (slavery, or the harshness of early capitalism) or their legacy in the present, but rather that it finds it impossible to respond to situations in which dramatic changes require new rules, and consequently some way of affecting an alteration of the approach to rule-making. In particular, it cannot respond to possibilities and problems raised by new technologies.

The problems inherent in the chief ways of assessing the legitimacy of rules—the liberal and the conservative approach—will thus become greater the more states try to protect their own citizens through the creation of social security measures; and the more technical or military change creates new challenges that seem to require rule-making responses. These two situations describe much of the world that globalization in practice continually creates. They explain in consequence the constant tendency to a self-subversion of the globalization process.

The Questioning of Rules in an Obscure
and Irregular System

THE CLASH of the large interpretative models or mental maps as set out in the previous chapter shapes our responses to the major international economic issues of the day. Globalization is quite an old phenomenon, as are the opposed ways of thinking about it. Disputes about global governance have, however, taken on a rather new dimension over the past half century of globalization—in other words, during the most recent (and the most rapid) wave of market integration. This is due mostly to changing expectations and demands about what states can and should do.

The growing complexity of law and rules, and the problems created by their continuous change and modification, is of course not a merely modern phenomenon. Gibbon's commentary on Justinian's codification of law is revealing:

> In a period of thirteen hundred years the laws had reluctantly followed the changes of government and manners; and the laudable desire of conciliating ancient names with recent institutions destroyed the harmony, and swelled the magnitude, of the obscure and irregular system. . . . But the government of Justinian united the evils of liberty and servitude, and the Romans were oppressed at the same time by the multiplicity of their laws and the arbitrary will of their master.[47]

Complexity often feels oppressive.

To the participants, cross-national market integration is an apparently chaotic process, which confuses many of those who are swept up by it. In particular, globalization subverts the political idea that characterized classic twentieth-century modernity, namely that the political process can determine social outcomes. Globalization is not obviously the consequence of any decision by particular powerful governments to embark on a strategy of globalization. Instead, governments usually see their role as reactive, a struggle to keep up with a changing and dynamic world that constantly changes the chances open to their citizens. They want to respond to demands that they should "do something." Many people instinctively think that they should subject the wild wave of globalization to checks and constraints. French politicians, in particular, have a whole theory on how a (feminine) globalization needs to be "mastered" (*maîtrisée*).[48] But how can this be done? And by whom?

In fact, any economic order does indeed depend on systems of rules to set a framework for the many millions of individual contracts that constitute the process of economic interaction. This is true on the international level as it is in national affairs. Globalization in fact requires rules. Its critics see rules as an expression of power relations. The problem for them lies in the way in which the rules are articulated.

Rules today are elaborated in a messy way. Modern rules do not appear on a stone tablet like the Ten Commandments. They are made as a result of a setting that in any national context is contested. The process of making and amending and extending rules encourages the formation of pressure and interest groups, which are continually trying to push the rule-based order in a way that favors their perceived interest. When rule-making is extended to an international level, there is a new round of clashes, in which the domestic interest groups try to dress their arguments up in the language of national interest.

Many analysts point out that international rules have a more flexible character than domestic law and that a useful distinction can be drawn between national government and international governance. Governments in this reading mostly welcome a governance that establishes incentives that make the world more stable and hence allow a more predictable base for policy-making.[49] But actually in many areas of economic rule-framing, international agreements act as an increasingly firm constraint on national legislation and on the decision-making and enforcing capability of states.

The most controversial current debates about the modern world economy concern the world trading system, the order of corporate governance, and the world monetary order. All of these domains have recently become highly contentious and politicized at the international level.

I

First, the commercial system is seen from two quite contrasting perspectives. In the "globalization" view of the world, trade wars are destructive and dangerous, reduce the possibility of prosperity, and lead to conflicts and clashes that may spill over into military conflict. The nightmare scenario is that of the U.S. Hawley-Smoot tariff, which came into effect in 1930, and played a major role in spreading the Great Depression, less because of its immediate effects than through the consequences of escalating retaliation in other countries. The post-1945 order evolved as a reaction based on lessons learned from the failures of the 1930s. Much of the postwar liberal order was inspired by a fundamentally simple perception of the U.S. secretary of state in the 1930s, Cordell Hull, who went back to the classical nineteenth-century British liberal certainties of Richard Cobden and John Bright. In explaining his proposal for reciprocal trade and tariff agreements, he told the House Committee, "International commerce conducted on a fair and mutually profitable basis, as this bill proposes, is not only calculated to aid materially in the restoration of prosperity everywhere, but it is the greatest civilizer and peacemaker in the experience of the human race."[50] Clause Four of the Atlantic Charter of 1941 stated that the wartime coalition would "further the enjoyment by all States, great or small, victor or vanquished, of access, on equal terms, to the trade and to the raw materials of the world." Treasury Secretary Henry Morgenthau started off the 1944 Bretton Woods conference by saying,

> Prosperity, like peace, is indivisible. We cannot afford to have it scattered here or there among the fortunate or to enjoy it at the expense of others. Poverty, where it exists, is menacing to us all and undermines the well-being of each of us. It can no more be localized than war, but spreads and saps the economic strength of all the more-favored areas of the earth.[51]

Globalizers are naturally relieved when states draw back from the brink of confrontation, as recently in the case of the U.S. steel tariffs dispute. They believe that the rationale for international economic institutions such as the GATT or the WTO lies in the enforcing of rules and procedures that might prevent the escalation of self-destructive responses to domestic political pressures. The likelihood of a WTO ruling against the steel tariffs thus recently helped the United States to have a better policy, and to give up on the unilateral imposition of the tariff. Rules will make the system work.

By contrast, the "imperialism" model thinks that trade relations shape an unequal system of exchange and dominance, and that political force molds trade law and patterns of commerce. Aggressive trade policy is or can be used as an instrument of policy and can create new opportunities for the assertion of power and the development of economic muscle. The current trade order thus reflects the ability of the United States to impose its vision on the world, and other countries are compelled or cajoled into compliance by threats (for instance to use Super 301 of the 1988 Trade and Competitiveness Act) or promises (of better access to U.S. markets). Rules are inherently and increasingly unfair.

Which of these views sits more firmly in the human psyche? One way of presenting the debate is in very simple terms, as a contest of emotion (fear and vulnerability) on the one side, and of reason and the willingness to accept uncontrolled events on the other. We are afraid that in commercial transactions in a non-ordered world we will be swindled. Others will take advantage of our ignorance or our weakness. In consequence, we can trade securely only with those we know well enough to trust. And they are likely to be nearer to us rather than far away. A long tradition, going back at least as far as Aristotle, consequently tells us that goods produced near home are better. The adage surfaces regularly: it told nineteenth-century Britons that they should not buy German seaside postcards or pianos, 1970s Americans that they should avoid Japanese cars, and Americans of the millennium that their Christmas celebrations should be purged of Chinese toys and decorations.

Alternately, we recognize that we cannot be self-sufficient and that we need to exchange. Where consumer habits are deeply entrenched, as they were in late-nineteenth-century Britain, and as they are in modern

America, the nativist appeal to fears about the malignancy of strangers falls mostly on deaf ears. After all, we do not expect to make our own pencils or grow our own food or weave and stitch our own clothing. The more we specialize and make particular products, the more we can trade and the wealthier we will become. Exchange is more likely to be effective and possible if there are stocks of goods, or a kind of capital. Such exchanges are not simply found among humans: male Antarctic penguins, for instance, build up stocks of pebbles, which they then use to trade for sex with female penguins who want them to build nests. Yet the exchange always raises questions of how the compact can be enforced, or how the partners can reasonably trust in the future performance of a contractual obligation. Fear of being swindled, or fear of commerce, is thus what stands in the way of realizing potential.

We might think that we can solve the dilemma by finding answers to three problems: first, fear is likely to be greater if markets are untransparent, when prices are not homogenous and cannot easily be compared, and when transactions are performed once only rather than repeated. So the more readily available the information, the less likely an anti-market backlash. But in a modern and complex economy the greater variety of goods and the more extended process of product differentiation can make prices more difficult to compare. The conquest of distance means that we are not dependent on doing business with nearby partners, and so transactions are not necessarily repeated as much as in the past. In a rapidly changing world, new patterns of commerce arise and will inevitably disrupt habitual arrangements in which partners have come over time to trust each other. Second, mistrust can have its origins in a psychology of fear. This is the sentiment that Franklin Roosevelt tried to banish during the Great Depression by claiming that the only thing we had to fear was fear itself. But fear increases with the perception that globalization is an uncontrollable process. Third, there is a fear of being disadvantaged by those with unequal market power, or greater wealth or capital. Increases in inequality that accompany the globalization process thus look as if they undermine the legitimacy of markets.

All these questions have in the past had political answers. These are problem areas where rules and their enforcement matter, and consequently where developments are driven by the logic of state action. Governments or intergovernmental organizations can facilitate access to information, raise confidence by regulations that forbid trading on the basis of privileged information ("insider dealing"), ensure that there are bigger and more regular markets, and use fiscal measures to redistribute wealth and remedy the inequality of market power.

The tension between, on the one side, a native suspicion of commerce and mistrust of long-distance anonymous dealings and, on the other, a wish to derive what in economists' jargon is called the "gains of trade" is an old one, but the kind of rules that evolved to make sure that trade is less harmful have changed quite dramatically.

In early modern Europe, or even in the nineteenth century, there were rules about trade, and there was trade policy on the part of the state (there was plenty of it), but there were no trade disputes in the modern sense of disputes between countries about how each should regulate its commerce. Trade policy largely meant protecting producers, whose output could be regarded as in some way (often a military way) necessary to the prosperity of the commonwealth. Agricultural producers, makers of iron and metal tools, suppliers of leather for army boots and belts, all could make this sort of argument. Security was the best way of dressing up claims to privileged protection. Even producers of the most exotically refined and completely unmilitary luxury goods—glassware, silks, and tapestries—however, presented an analogous case and found that states protected them.

Disputes arising in regard to individual problematic trades could be regulated in exactly the same manner as disputes over domestic trade. There were plenty of legal cases that spanned across national boundaries: supposing a German merchant did not receive payment for goods promised by an Argentine importer? Since transactions such as these were in the nineteenth century usually financed by bills drawn on banks in the City of London, a British court would arbitrate on the dispute. These, however, were affairs of courts, not affairs of parliaments or politicized legislatures. Trade depended on mechanisms to ensure that contracts were enforced, and hence more widespread commerce demanded the evolution of a legal culture.[52]

With such a culture in place, it became thinkable for states to make commitments through negotiated treaties about the removal of restraints and protection. In the middle of the nineteenth century a general movement to liberalize trade followed the British abolition of the Corn Laws in 1846. The result divided politics along lines corresponding to particular sectors of the economy, with consumers of imports, including many manufacturers, demanding liberalization against the opposition of domestic producers. When continental European countries concluded trade treaties with Great Britain or with each other, which usually included a Most-Favored-Nation (MFN) clause to extend the concessions mutually made in other trade agreements, they generally provoked a considerable and organized opposition of manufacturers who stood to lose from more competition with more efficient British producers. The canonical European text for opposition to free trade became a work written by the German Friedrich List, *The National System of Political Economy*, in which he defended the notion that "infant industries" needed to be protected while they were developing against a ruinous competition that would wipe out the later basis for prosperity. List described the ascendancy of English ideas—"Manchesterism"—as a device that Britain was using to kick away a ladder that would prevent other countries from ascending the scale of wealth by progressively improving their manufactures. "In Adam Smith's time, a new maxim was for the first time added . . . namely, to conceal the true policy of England under the cosmopolitan expressions and arguments which Adam Smith had discovered, in order to induce foreign nations not to imitate that policy."[53] List's counterpart across the Atlantic was Alexander Hamilton in his 1791 *Report on Manufactures*.

Pressure from interests badly affected by alterations in trade policy built up, because there was no obvious legal reason why states could not change their policy stance. A new domain of choice in policy thus gave rise to a new sort of politics, in which parties defined themselves very simply in terms of interests, the "manufacturing interest", or the "country interest." There was no compulsion arising out of any kind of international consideration for countries to conclude free trade agreements, or to maintain the levels of tariff that they had when they accepted a MFN clause. Indeed, from the 1870s, the continental European countries, under heavy pressure from manufacturing lobby groups, stepped back from open trade and imposed protectionist tariff legislation. The United States, easily the most successful industrializing economy of the nineteenth century, never participated in the move to open trade, and its dynamism looked like a striking vindication of the Listian principle. By the end of the nineteenth century, many countries added non-tariff restrictions: in particular politically sensitive sectors of the economy such as agriculture could be effectively protected by hygiene and veterinary regulation. All of these measures could be, and were, fiercely debated in domestic political settings. They could also provoke international political tension: Russian-German relations took an initial knock in the 1880s when German cereal tariffs seemed to exclude Russia's most successful export from a large industrialized market. Russia had no legal case against Germany, however, and Russian noblemen could not sue Bismarck or German consumers for not importing Russian grain.

By the beginning of the twentieth century, as increased trade as well as flows of migrant workers changed relative incomes, workers whose wages were eroded started to put forward a new sort of argument: that some kinds of imports were "unfair" because they reflected the outcome of policy in other countries that allowed a subsidization of export producers at the cost of domestic consumers. Germany thus sold steel and ships at lower prices abroad than at home; and German exporters drew on a powerful network of sales support from German consulates all over the world.[54] Low-cost producers, in India and Japan, were also denounced as "unfair competitors." When these anxieties were coupled with fears about security and about German power, trade could be discussed in a new language. In 1916, for example, the U.S. Congress passed the Anti-Dumping Law. Above all, there seemed to be a new logic that required concerted international action. In 1919, during the Paris Peace Conference, American labor unions pressed vigorously for a new institution, the International Labour Organisation, that would stem the tide of low-cost textiles from Asia.

Twentieth-century clashes about trade thus turned to the issue of rules about rules: in short, a higher dimension of rule-making. What sort of national policy might be permissible, and what needed to be banned? And how could a ban be enforced?

This new dimension in international regulation paralleled the working out of domestic agendas about appropriate trade policy. The assertion of power interests, at least superficially, looks like the most plausible account of how modern trade negotiations work. Economists often find it hard to explain why countries do not simply unilaterally adopt free trade policies, since this would produce overall benefits that outweighed the costs that would hit some sectors. The answer lies in the power of particular interests to organize and impose their preferences through the political process. Legislatures are particularly open to this kind of pressure, since individual representatives will have close ties to particular localities where a particular interest is concentrated. The result is that the legislature simply accumulates (or "log rolls") sectional interests. A classic work of political science, Elmer Schattschneider's *Politics, Pressures and the Tariff*, indeed demonstrated how it was exactly this mechanism that had turned a modest proposal for raised protection for agriculture made by Herbert Hoover during the 1928 presidential campaign, into the destructive Hawley-Smoot tariff of 1930 with its 21,000 separate tariff positions. A later formulation, by Mancur Olson, distinguished between sectional interests, which are strong, and an encompassing interest, which may be represented only weakly.[55]

Hawley-Smoot was quickly viewed as a catastrophe, and seen as a major cause of the collapse of world trade and hence of the Great Depression. The remedies in trade policy involved first strengthening the executive relative to the legislature, and second, proceeding to the negotiation of bilateral tariff reductions. These two steps were indeed packaged by Roosevelt's secretary of state, Cordell Hull. He was regularly portrayed by his critics as a rather ineffective mono-maniac, but is now widely recognized as the architect of the trading system of the second half of the twentieth century, and thus the initiator of a period of unparalleled and worldwide prosperity. The Reciprocal Trade Agreements Act (RTAA) of 1934 gave the administration authority to negotiate bilateral agreements. In the course of domestic discussions over such negotiations, it became easier for the interests that stood to gain from trade opening to make their cases and thus block suboptimal and protectionist outcomes.

The postwar trading system was initially rather provisional, in that the planned International Trade Organization was never realized. The GATT was a framework within which many bilateral pairs of negotiations could be conducted, and their results then multilateralized. The negotiating mechanism thus retained the characteristic approach of the RTAA. Later rounds of GATT discussions, in particular the Kennedy and the Tokyo Rounds, evolved into genuine multilateral approaches to tariff reduction.

The privatization of trade negotiations, which the shift to the RTAA and the GATT had been intended to counter, emerged again in the 1970s when macroeconomic instability as well as increased internationalization threatened entrenched interests. The most obvious reflection of the new-found power of private interests came in the U.S. Trade Act of 1974. Section 301 allowed industries that believed themselves victims of dumping by foreign exporters to present a case.

In 1995 the World Trade Organization was created as the product of the last and most complex round of GATT negotiations (the Uruguay Round). It was much obviously closer to the ideal of rules, with its own arbitration and dispute settlement procedure. Yet the WTO rapidly became politicized in a way that the GATT had generally managed to avoid. In part this happened because the WTO became a much bigger organization: whereas the GATT had started in 1948 with 22 "contracting parties" or members, and had increased to 123 by 1994, the WTO in 2005 has 148 members. In part, the politicization was a consequence of the extension of the agenda during the intense debates that had preceded the creation of the new institution. During the debates over the NAFTA, U.S. President Clinton had made a commitment to include labor and environmental issues. The result was that there was a presumption that such issues should also be included in the operation of a new global trade institution.

The WTO proceedings were also more open than GATT negotiations, with the result that the positions of the various parties could be well known in advance, and subjected to the lobbying of trade interest groups. Domestic politics could easily intrude into the process. The Seattle meeting of the WTO (2000) became the subject of a rancorous debate. At the level of popular politics, the meeting was followed with a degree of intensity that differed radically from the obscure and unpublicized days of GATT. The negotiators had to operate in near-siege conditions as anti-WTO protesters wanted to protest against the "unfairness" of world trade. At the level of the negotiations themselves, the United States was generally blamed for the failure of the session, because of its endorsement of a labor rights and environmental agenda that many developing countries felt to be a dressed-up version of old protectionism aimed primarily against their industrialization strategies.

Obviously, there are other reasons why trade issues since the 1990s have become more contentious and capable of wreaking large-scale damage to the idea of international community: reasons that have nothing to do with the intrinsic trade issues themselves. In the Cold War, there were plenty of large-scale clashes over trade between the United States and its allies: for instance, the "chicken war" with Europe in the 1960s, struggles with Japan over automobiles in the 1970s, and semiconductors in the 1980s, or the almost permanent tussles with Europe over agricultural tariffs and farm support. These spats, however, were not allowed to escalate into divisions that threatened the alliance, because the politicians who saw themselves as big boys or grown-ups in the foreign ministries and prime ministers' offices did not want to see basic principles of national security undermined by low-level trade negotiators. By contrast, after 1989–90, there was little really to fear from political conflict, and the clashes could become poisonous and corrosive.

The external framework is not enough, however, to explain the severity of the current difficulties. One of the ways that power relations look more obvious in the trade framework today is a consequence of both the development of big corporate interests and the way in which trade rules have become very complicated and specific, and thus easily bent in the direction of particular interests. There is a long history behind this development. Part of the political compromise behind the reorientation of American trade policy in the 1930s involved the insight that in domestic politics, industries that would benefit from access to foreign markets would have a motivation to lobby for reciprocal trade agreements. The resulting clash of corporate interests over trade policy might push in the direction of liberalization, rather than log-rolling protection as in the process described by Schattschneider.[56] It also led to the expansion of the types of activity covered by trade talks. In particular, as the strengths of the U.S. economy shifted away from manufacturing, producers of services began to ask why a worldwide liberalization for services could not be negotiated as part of a deal in which foreign manufacturers would have greater access to U.S. markets. A number of powerful financial services companies, in particular American Express, the insurer American International Group or AIG, and Citibank, in 1982 formed the Coalition of Service Industries to press for the extension of trade agreements into the service sector, on the grounds that this was where American companies and American interests had a strategic advantage in the world.[57]

The new corporate bargaining within sectors and industries provided as much of the dynamism for trade opening as did the public relations façade used by executives when they claimed to represent an overarching or encompassing interest to promote the open world trading system. It had one obvious disadvantage, though, in that it made a clear identification of national policy with the particular sectoral interests of important producers. So trade disputes could become gladiatorial matches of big corporations. Trade policy looked more and more as if it was captured by interests.

The process of capture is much easier in the case of some particularly sensitive products, which have an aura of importance and significance about them: they are, in a common phrase, "too important to be left to the market." In areas such as food or aerospace or energy, the idea of a strategic good with a particular claim to national attention remains particularly powerful. Sometimes this argument is backed up by an argument about the desirability of securing rents that follow from a peculiar price structure: whereby "strategic trade theory" explains that an industry with very high and lumpy investment costs can be developed with protection and then become a practical monopolist because of the extent of the research and start-up costs. It is in these cases that the impulse to redefine rules in the interests of power and politics is most developed.

The case of food subsidies in the major industrial countries—in the European Union, the United States, and in Japan—is a notorious stumbling block to greater liberalization of world trade. The capacity to escalate food trade conflicts into major clashes reached well beyond goods that play a major role in a national economy. How can the definition of a banana be used to promote the products of a particular area controlled by a particular company? One of the most celebrated trade disputes of the 1990s was the banana war, when the European Union adopted a policy of preferences for the products of sixty-nine

African-Caribbean-Pacific countries that was ruled in 1997 to be incompatible with WTO rules. The countries that were hurt most by the
regime were major Latin American producers, but the case was brought
to the WTO by the United States, largely as a result of the lobbying of
the company Chiquita, which had invested large resources in developing products for an E.U. market that it had mistakenly believed was
about to be liberalized. The case—which developed in parallel with EU
resistance to hormonally treated beef, and to genetically modified food-
stuffs—in which the same sort of intense lobbying by particular U.S.
corporations was highly visible, convinced many Europeans that the
whole edifice of trade negotiations was simply a corporate political
playball.[58]

Aerospace, in which there are only a very few large producers, lends
itself to the extension of interest politics. There is a military link, in that
civilian manufacturers also have a major role in military supply. Some
products for the civilian market can be diverted to military demand.
The normally rational and moderate commentator Robert Samuelson
(though admitting that this was an "awful solution") recently called for
a boycott of Airbus products; if American airlines neglected their patri-
otic duty to buy American, they should be constrained by congressional
action.[59]

The most strikingly politicized twentieth-century product, however, is
petroleum. Control of oil fields already played a major role in the formulation of war aims in World War I. In the domestic context, the resource
curse of oil revenues produced struggles for control and authoritarian
politics in the Middle East, Venezuela, Nigeria, and post-communist Russia. In international politics, the oil price became a proxy for the degree
of politicization of the international economy in the last half of the twentieth century. When the oil price was low and falling in real terms, in the
1950s and 1960s, the availability of cheap energy fueled the growth of international trade; but it also made for a lower level of conflict.

In the 1970s, with the major oil price increases of 1973–74 and
1979–80, the whole trading system was threatened. In the 1980s and
1990s, world trade expanded and trade liberalization advanced with
falling oil prices. After 2000, increased oil prices have directly indicated
the way in which strategic thinking comes back into the economic debate. The initial price rise directly reflected the outbreak of the second

51

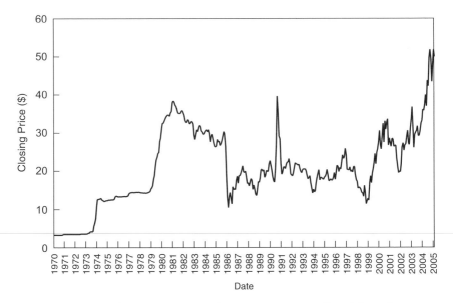

2 Daily closing oil price, 1970–2005 (West Texas Intermediate $/barrel)

Palestinian intifada. China, in particular, growing very quickly, and with a sharply rising demand for oil, acquired the physical resources of oil fields (with the Sinupec group developing the Iranian Yadavarn field, while the China National Petroleum Corporation acquired a stake in the major Russian oil and gas group), built pipelines to Central Asia, and made shipping facilities a major policy goal. The government formulated what it termed a "go out" strategy, in which China cooperated in oil exploration with twenty-seven countries, with payment through concessional loans, as in Angola, or through $15 billion worth of debt relief for Sudan. While the market could be relied on to sell the products of China's dynamic new industries, it could not be a secure vehicle of providing energy.

The Chinese path looks very much like a reprise of earlier actions by economically dynamic states that worried about the security of oil supplies. These states thought that the market was too vulnerable to disruption and that instead they should rely on powerful and notionally private corporations as a way of enforcing their power interests—Britain through the Anglo-Iranian Oil Company, which clashed spectacularly with the Iranian government in the early 1950s; or the United

States through Aramco, a consortium controlled by Texaco and Standard Oil of California, in the case of Saudi petroleum. Since the big clashes of the 1970s, however, the United States began to rely more on the market. At that time, the key insight of the Western governments' response to the big oil price increases was that oil producers would be lured back into the system by the logic of their own financial interests. Oil producers would not be able immediately to spend the additional revenues that followed from the price rise, and the reinvesting (the so-called "recycling" of petro-dollars) would tie the producers to the well-being of the international order as it was. The market in other words began to appeal as an instrument of the "West." Precisely for these reasons, China at the beginning of the twenty-first century is suspicious of it.

In the ancien régime world of mercantilist policies, trade control was justified by security. In the modern world economy, many commodities are left to the market, but not those that are thought to be central to power relations. The struggle for control over these strategic goods means a continual spilling of power into the arena of rules. Mercantilism exercises a continued attraction.

II

The discussion of trade issues indicates the extent to which the market has been overshadowed by the idea that politics is driven by particular corporate strategies to control particular markets. Secondly, then, corporate governance has become a contested area in international economic relations, shaped by national politics and national preference formulation. Accounting standards raise the issue of how to determine the worth of companies, and hence of how stock markets can assess stock market performance, and how investors can allocate resources most rationally. A struggle between the U.S. method, based on Generally Agreed Accounting Principles (GAAPs), and the European International Accounting Standards, is thus widely seen as a fight for which companies can attract capital and grow.

Corporate governance until very recently was thought to be strictly the domain of national governments and regulators. As in the case of trade law, this does not mean that until then international considerations played no role in shaping national political approaches to legislation. On the contrary, nation-states tried to export their preferences and impose them on their neighbors. As with trade, in the pre-modern era, public institutions dealt with companies and treated them with a great deal of suspicion, aiming to restrict their activities.

Early modern European states in general were quite weak, and found mercantile ventures threatening, especially when they crossed state borders. Some companies or corporations (in today's discourse they might be regarded as nongovernmental organizations or NGOs) behaved like states without actually being territorial states. The Teutonic Knights and the Knights of Malta organized defense systems, fostered commerce, provided social networks and services (such as hospitals or schools), and, of course, did a great deal of fighting. These were proto-NGOs, dedicated to a cause that was overwhelmingly important to their adherents (a religious crusade). Larger companies had to act in an analogous way.

The great merchant companies of early modern Europe indeed had their own armies: the most notorious examples are the French and the English East India Companies. The British East India Company indeed had an important army at a time when British political life resulted in the crown (i.e., the state) not having a standing army at all. The companies took on regulatory and quasi-state powers with which they could exclude any competition: they were conceived as monopoly corporations. Political pressure flowed from protests against such privileged private corporations, and erupted in the American and French revolutions. The debate produced a new type of state: a state that because it derived its legitimacy from popular will ("We the people . . . .") would deal with companies and non-state actors in a very different way. The state after the French Revolution would claim a moral superiority in dealing with business corporations, instead of seeing itself as simply a party to a transaction that could be more-or-less cynically calculated (as was the Emperor Charles V in his sixteenth-century dealings with the banker Jakob Fugger).

It is a crude fallacy to think that the development and growth of the state necessarily brings disadvantages for enterprise or business culture. On the contrary, to the extent that the strengthening of the state made business life much more predictable, wealth generation became easier.

If the competition among European states made for more dynamic business life, the constitutional ordering of the popular will made life more certain. Previous monarchical borrowers had been prone to sudden bankruptcy, and the Habsburg and Valois dynasts regularly turned on their creditors and used force (the threat of execution for usury) to renegotiate on better terms.[60]

The business response to this was one of grateful relief. As long as conditions were stable, it made sense to respect the will of the people as expressed in a systematically and constitutionally ordered way in whatever state a company did business. By the early nineteenth century, some large-scale lenders such as the Rothschilds began to insist that their customer states introduce constitutions or representative assemblies, because this made the repayment of credit more secure.[61] This was a foreign policy driven entirely by self-interest, but it was of course also a highly enlightened one. This point that businesses should be "good citizens" has actually become something of a platitude.

The citizenship of business corporations, however, became deeply problematical in the course of the twentieth century. Here are quotations from two mid-twentieth-century business leaders that may strike the reader as utterly unremarkable, so banal that it may even be a waste of time discussing them in an arena where we should be thinking about issues that are contentious and problematical.

(1): It is evident that a company which operates in a country where it is accepted and whose laws guarantee its protection has to be [unconditionally] loyal to that country and has to conscientiously comply with its wishes.[62]

(2): Now I believe that if an international business such as General Motors engages in the commercial activity of any country with the idea of making a profit . . . it has an obligation to that country, both in an economic sense as well perhaps as in a social sense. It should attempt to attune itself to the general business of the community; make itself a part of the same; conduct its operations in relation to the customs, and design its products so as to meet the needs and viewpoint of each community, so far as it can. I believe further, that that should be its position, even if, as is likely to happen and particularly as was the case during the past few years, the management of the Corporation might not wholly agree with many things that are done in certain of these countries.[63]

What is surprising is not that these sentiments were expressed, but the circumstances in which they came. Does the doctrine of "good citizenship" mean that companies should accept any political regime in which they do business, however odious? The context of the two quotations was, in the first instance, Max Huber—the chairman of the Supervisory Board of a Swiss company, the Rheinfelden aluminum works (AIAG), which owned substantial production facilities in Germany—writing in the introduction to an official company history in 1942. Huber was also the president of the International Committee of the Red Cross, and the ICRC behaved during the World War II with the same kind of accomodating logic that made it reluctant to discuss publicly or to condemn outrages witnessed directly or indirectly by its representatives. This action, or rather lack of it, justified in the name of good citizenship, led to substantial and, in my view, justified criticism of the ICRC after the war.

The second extract is from a letter of Alfred Sloan, the chief executive of General Motors, to a shareholder worried about the company's German subsidiary in the Nazi era. Perhaps these are both quite exceptional circumstances.

These episodes demonstrate very dramatically that states cannot always be relied upon to be "good." The greatest problem of today is how and by what standards can companies, or indeed NGOs, criticize and intervene in the affairs of states, which when under attack like to remind critics of the international law notion of "sovereignty".

In a world in which there is dramatic political or military conflict among states, states themselves will intervene to stop businesses acting promiscuously as good citizens in countries that the state considers hostile or threatening. States rather than companies would then decide on an appropriate foreign policy. This was, or might have been, the best answer to the World War II dilemma of companies doing business with the Nazis: governments, even of neutral countries, might have forbidden commerce (as did the United States in June 1941 in the case of U.S. corporations, six months before its entry into the war). The Swiss problem was that the government did not provide correct guidelines about corporate action, and indeed in some cases provided credit to Swiss firms that were trading with Nazi Germany.

Governments thus regulated their businesses (which they wanted to see as national businesses) and subjected them to the control of national policy. Such an approach, however, contains potential clashes when business became internationalized, and the regulation of business would bring about the competition of states and the values and interests that they see themselves as embodying. New attempts at the generation of common standards also clearly reflect a world in which corporate activity is not confined to national frontiers. A recent example of how hard it is for corporations to span transatlantic differences about values comes from Wal-Mart. As service industries become more globalized, the question of the transfer of values from one country with different social patterns to another becomes more complex. The giant U.S. retailer Wal-Mart not only struck its European employees as overly prudish when, in reaction to an American debate about proper standards of workplace behavior, it issued a long memorandum to accompany every pay check banning romantic relationships among its staff. The company's German employees claimed that the document was actually a violation of German law, in that the General Works Council was only informed about the new policy, but had not been given its legally guaranteed opportunity to discuss and modify it.[64]

The first area where the new problems of regulating cross-national business became really evident came as a result of the development of higher levels of capital mobility. As international capital markets took off in the 1970s, some international institutions as well as the Federal Reserve Board chairman, Arthur Burns, called for some regulation of cross-border activities; but the demand was not translated into systematic discussions until the major Latin American debt crisis of 1982, which for a time appeared to threaten the stability of the financial systems in lending countries. As part of a bill approving an IMF quota increase to deal with the aftermath of the debt crisis, the U.S. Congress passed the International Lending Supervision Act in November 1983, which required American regulators to seek a convergence of international bank capital standards. By 1988 a set of standards known as the Basle Accord had been evolved by the major industrial countries. The 1988 Accord looked outdated even at the time of its implementation in that it rested on a very simple division of country risk by whether or not the country was a member of the OECD. Producing a revised agreement proved to be a very time-consuming activity, but also a very controversial one. The new proposed Basle Accord provided for a number of alternative options, including letting banks' own sophisticated financial models; but at the last minute, in 2004, the United States announced that it would consider applying the new capital adequacy standards only to its internationally operating banks, so that there might be a protected domestic sector.

There are also obvious overlaps between corporate governance and issues concerned with trade law, and between these and financial stability issues. Already before the 1997–98 Asia financial crisis, the U.S. Treasury and American banking interests were pressing Asian countries to open up their financial markets, treating this as an issue primarily concerned with the liberalization of trade in services (rather than as a matter of financial stability). The major rationalization was that an entry of foreign firms would lead to quite dramatic efficiency and productivity gains.[65] A 1996 Treasury memorandum as summarized in the *New York Times* stated, "Priority areas where Treasury is seeking further liberalization . . . included letting foreigners buy domestic Korean bonds; letting Korean companies borrow abroad both short term and long term; and letting foreigners buy Korean stock more easily . . . These are all of interest to the U.S. financial services community."[66] In the wake of the Asia crisis, international institutions and the U.S. government focused much of their analysis on misgovernance or "crony capitalism" as responsible for the crises in Asian economies. According to this analysis, crony capitalism had led to a misinvestment in unproductive enterprises, and to moral hazard problems. International lenders and investors had chosen to lend by preference to borrowers who were politically well connected, and whose debts thus carried an implicit government guarantee. Any reform program thus required a dismantling of corrupt structures and the institution of accounting and oversight mechanisms to guarantee greater corporate transparency.

The most contentious issue in the Doha Round of trade negotiations concerned rules for investment, which were often seen by developing countries as a way of producing one-sided benefits for industrial capital-exporting countries and interests. The tough position adopted by Japan and the European Union on investment rules (the so-called Singapore issues) was largely responsible for the breakdown of the Cancun ministerial meeting of the WTO.

In analyzing governance, it is hard to separate concern with overall rules from debates about self-interest—whether with the discussion of trade-related investment issues, or with the dismantling of crony capitalism. Critics pointed out that, in practice, improved transparency in domestic financial systems meant permitting market entry to large U.S. and E.U. institutions. American banks took dominant positions in Mexico and Korea, and Spanish banks in South America. After big corporate scandals emerged in the United States and other big industrial countries, much of the 1997–98 preaching to Asia looked outrageously hypocritical. Again, it could be portrayed easily as a mask for concrete interests and for the projection of power.

The aftermath of 1997–98 also demonstrated in a new way the vulnerability of the modern transnational corporation, especially in newer (and nonmanufacturing) sectors of the economy. A worldwide manufacturing company, such as Singer Sewing Machines or International Harvester in the early twentieth century, or even like IBM in its heyday, can maintain its reputation by paying attention to quality in its products, and to a high standard of service for complicated and easily broken equipment. Product quality in manufacturing can more easily be controlled from the corporate headquarters than can the skill-intensive service industries that characterize the most recent development of the world economy.

The most obvious corporate solution to the perceived problem of the 1990s, that emerging markets suffered most from an underendowed and underskilled financial sector, was to transplant best-practice American (and to some extent European) banks. So institutions such as Citibank (later Citigroup) became the embodiment of a new philosophy of management. In practice, however, such global institutions need to recruit a substantial amount of local labor, because they are, after all, working in a local setting and they become vulnerable as every misstep reflects not only locally but also worldwide on a global brand. The brand depended on the ability of the innovator to supply a more sophisticated and well-controlled approach to the management of financial systems. Thus Citibank was seen by policy reformers as the ideal institutional rescue for Mexico's ramshackle financial system after the crisis of 1994–95, or for Korea after 1997–98. Yet Citibank rapidly became tainted by quite particular small-scale problems that reflected on its global philosophy of management. A big corruption scandal erupted around its private bank in Mexico; investigations after August 2001 by the Japanese Financial Services Agency led to complaints about making loans for the manipulation of stock, about assistance in the misrepresentation of profits, and about failure to check new customers for criminal backgrounds; major losses occurred in Argentina after 2001; and in 2004 the German financial market regulator Bafin complained that Citigroup had flooded the bond market with 11 billion Euros in bonds that distorted the market and created big losses for other market-makers. The architects of the European bond scheme allegedly dubbed it "Dr. Evil." Reacting to the Japanese scandal, the bank commissioned a report by a former U.S. comptroller of the currency, Eugene Ludwig, who concluded, "In hindsight, one may fairly question whether global business and international supervision was close enough to recognize the severity of the management discord in Japan." The new chief executive of Citigroup responded by recognizing that his institution had "chewed up the franchise" in pursuit of short-term profits. "It's our fault, because all we talk about is delivering the numbers. We've done this for ever."[67]

In a sort of cyclical development, the modern corporation looked as if it had the same problems of overreach and at the same time the global vulnerability of the early modern trading companies. Thus the same issues about regulation that arose in the national context of pre–French Revolutionary Europe appear on the international level. They seem hard to solve: even in the very well-integrated European Union, banking regulation is a national not a European function; and those who try to defend this apparent failure of institutions resort to making a point about an even more absurd situation in the United States, where insurance is regulated at the state rather than the federal level.

There might be two solutions to the modern dilemma, though each raises new and considerable problems. A more intense institutionalization of the international order could secure more transparency and more immunity from domestic and particular pressures. Secondly, the issues of corporate governance could be managed through a higher reliance on law and a judicial approach, which increasingly moves across national frontiers. Regulators may still be very national, but courts are prepared to engage in an aggressive conquest of new territory.

The first approach brings a new layer of control over corporate life. Over the past ten years, there has been a systematic attempt to engage international institutions in governance issues. This is partly because the legal framework of a modern economy is so complex that it would be needlessly and senselessly complicated for national governments to work out all the rules required from scratch. In practice, when many states adopted market economies in the aftermath of the collapse of communism, they almost invariably followed either the legal systems of the European Community/European Union or of the United States.[68]

The movement of international institutions to an intense concern with corporate governance is in part a response to the development of the transnational corporation; but it is also the product of an intellectual shift. For most of the post-1945 period, theories of development were spelled out in very simple macroeconomic terms, in particular about the need to shift more resources to investment. In the past twenty years, the focus shifted because of a recognition that large amounts of investment alone do not guarantee development, and that investment may be misinvestment. Microeconomic arguments about efficiency took the place of honor previously held by the big (mostly Keynesian) macroeconomic approaches. In thinking about efficiency, corporate governance is a significant determinant.

During and after the Asia crisis, the World Bank and the International Monetary Fund actively pushed for large-scale structural reform, which they included in their policy conditionality. The most famously interventionist of the programs involved dealing with Indonesia, which was in political transition with the collapse of the authoritarian Suharto regime. The specific points of the Indonesia program looked surprisingly detailed to people accustomed to thinking of the IMF as an institution concerned with big macroeconomic fundamentals. For instance,

> Effective February 1, 1998, traders will have the freedom to buy, sell, and transfer all commodities across district and provincial boundaries, including cloves, cashew nuts, oranges, and vanilla. In particular, traders will be able to buy and sell cloves at unrestricted prices to all agents, effective immediately, and the Clove Marketing Board will be eliminated by June 1998.

Many of the most controversial micro-interventions of the IMF were aimed at dismantling parts of the patronage and clientage networks of

Suharto. Thus as part of its program, the IMF asked for the ending of the clove monopoly, which had been not only essential to the manufacture of the ubiquitous kretek cigarettes, but also, in fact, the mainstay of the regime's influence. The IMF also insisted on the closing of sixteen insolvent banks in November 1997, a move that critics claimed worsened the financial panic.[69]

At the same time, such demands looked as if they constituted interventions to change the balance of national power: to acquire advantages for U.S. corporations, which might acquire assets at fire-sale bargain-basement post-crisis prices. The international solutions thus became entangled not just in the webs of domestic politics, but in the conflicting webs of national corporate politics originating out of two very different systems, American and Asian Corporate reform as a solution to the Asia crisis thus could be presented by critics such as Mahathir Mohamad as an anti-Asian drive, rather than as a solution to a generalized problem of bad corporate governance. The search for rules was advantaging particular interests.

The second solution to the modern problem, to involve courts, also raises questions of power reaching beyond territorial boundaries. Instead of international institutions becoming enmeshed in rival versions of corporate governance preferences, there is a clash of courts coming from different political orders. When companies are owned by nationals of many countries, listed on several stock exchanges, and do business globally, it is rarely clear where legal issues can be properly concluded or settled.

A particularly dramatic instance of how power politics interact with corporate reform is the saga of the Russian oil company Yukos. Given the capacity of raw materials to generate highly lucrative rents, it is probably not surprising that the most extreme examples of power intrusions occur in the energy sector. President Putin presented the Russian government's campaign to seize and sell Yukos assets to pay tax liabilities as part of a war against oligarchs, who in the 1990s had manipulated and distorted the Russian political process. The major accusation against the head of Yukos, Mikhail Khodorkovsky, was that as chairman of the Menatep commercial bank in 1994 he had mounted a conspiracy to pervert the process of privatization of Russian state assets. The arrest of Khodorkovsky was simply a Russian counterpart to investigations of corporate malfeasance elsewhere in the world, of Enron, Worldcom, or Parmalat. Yukos's defenders, on the other hand, depicted the government's action as simply an unscrupulous raiding of assets in a truly ancien régime manner that was endangering the rule of property rights, and thus the basis of the Russian transition to capitalism and the rule of law. The affair, however, was not a Russian one alone, in that some 15 percent of Yukos was owned by American investors, who would take their case to a court in Texas. From the Russian government's perspective, the same international game could be played, of asserting national jurisdiction in order to build national advantages. It proceeded to treat the issue as one regulated solely by Russian law. The partial resale of Yukos assets and their renationalization to Yuganskneftegas at the end of 2004 was financed by a German bank, in the wake of a highly publicized visit of Putin with German Chancellor Gerhard Schröder; and some 20 percent of the new company was sold to the China National Petroleum Corporation, on the grounds given by a Kremlin analyst that "the offer . . . is a clear signal of Russia's disappointment with the U.S. and Europe."[70]

Disputes about different codes of corporate governance, about accountancy rules, and about the applicability of commercial law codes drawn from different national legislative traditions, all are struggles in which there are muscular demands for the assertion of power interests. Instead of legal stability, a clash of different legal cultures and traditions of corporate regulation has begun to be treated as simply part of the grand bargaining of international politics. So rules look quite arbitrary or indeed ruleless.

III

Third, investment flows produce discussion about the monetary transfer of assets and values, and hence about the way in which they can be regulated or controlled. The international monetary order is sucked into the debate about corporate governance, but more generally about politics and power.

In the "globalization" interpretation, the operation of the international economy requires a stable system of monetary rules. Such a system clearly may take quite a broad diversity of forms. The restoration of the world monetary order after the breakdown of the interwar era and the World War II took place on the basis of fixed exchange rates and restrictions on capital mobility. A comprehensive system of rules was created in the postwar world. Modern globalization has developed on the basis of flexible exchange rates among major industrial economies and on capital mobility, as a result of the legal document behind the 1944 arrangement, the IMF Articles of Agreement, having been amended to oblige members of the Fund "to assure orderly exchange arrangements and to promote a stable system of exchange rates." Yet both these monetary orders, the fixed exchange rate regime and a "stable" system of flexible rates as provided by the 1976 Second Amendment of the Articles of Agreement, are internally consistent and robust.

The "imperialist" vision takes these rules and sees political advantage lurking behind them, manipulating their application. Both the Bretton Woods system (the first postwar order of fixed exchange rates) and the modern international economy gave the United States an unfair position. Although the first American drafts proposed a new international unit of account as the basis of the postwar monetary system, the chief American negotiator, Harry Dexter White, at an early stage made it clear that he thought that in reality the U.S. dollar "will probably be the cornerstone of the postwar structure of stable currencies."[71] In their original form, the IMF Articles of Agreement correspondingly required member countries to fix their currencies in terms of gold or the U.S. dollar. From an early moment, there were major outflows of investment funds from the United States, but they corresponded to a buildup of short-term assets as well as physical currency outside the United States. This fact provoked the accusation that the United States and U.S. multinationals were achieving global economic dominance without really paying a price, since the reserve holdings of other countries were in practice financing American acquisitions.

The explicit discussions of the problems of international rule-making are again, as in the case of the discussion of trade conflicts or of differing views of corporate governance, quite recent. The underlying problems are not. Particularly in the monetary domain, the arguments are often cast with a nostalgic look back at the gold standard, which is supposed to have been the rule that underpinned the nineteenth- and early-twentieth-century push to globalization. The gold standard and an idea of British hegemony are usually associated; and London was the undisputed financial center of the pre–1914 world. At the beginning of the nineteenth century, Britain together with its oldest ally, the rather economically insignificant Portugal, were the only countries on a gold standard. By the end of the nineteenth century, all the major powers operated a gold standard, and those countries left on a silver standard (Mexico and China) were thought to be rather anomalous. The result was that the gold standard was portrayed as marching hand in hand with the triumph of Manchesterism.

In fact, the gold standard was an international system, but it was not a generally agreed-upon rule about the homogenization of money and currencies. There had been an attempt at this, in 1867, when Napoleon III convened in Paris an International Monetary Conference that he and his advisers believed would settle the question of the monetary standard and introduce a world currency.[72] Given only relatively small alterations of the exchange rates, it would have been possible to bring the franc, which was widely used in western and southern Europe, the British pound, and the American dollar together, since a dollar was worth almost five francs in gold, and a pound twenty-five (or five dollars). Almost, but not quite: the scheme failed because the British government feared the outcry that a small alteration of the metallic equivalent of the pound would have brought. The gold standard was thus not a generally agreed upon international standard: instead, as Kenneth Dam points out, "it rested fundamentally upon domestic law in each of the principal trading nations."[73]

When analysts look at the practical operation of the gold standard, they are surprised at how little attention the central banks at the center of the system's operation gave to international issues. The major task of the central bank was running discount policy: setting interest rates so that there was sufficient liquidity for the operation of commerce, but without such abandon that the gold stock of the central bank would be threatened by the volume of bills circulating. It did not, as Karl Polanyi misleadingly described it, produce an outcome in which "under nineteenth century conditions foreign trade and the gold standard had undisputed priority over the needs of domestic business."[74] The cooperative elements of the system, and the extent of international binding, were astonishingly slight until 1890; and cooperation blossomed only in what were in fact the last years of the gold standard, at a time when international relations generally were worsening in the lead up to World War I.[75]

The central belief of the order was also not at all concerned with any international rule or mechanism: no one would want to defend gold or discount policies by stating that "the international system requires us to do this." Instead, the core psychological belief worked because enough people believed that gold was the most obvious and the most appropriate store of value. This was not just an abstract belief: gold coins circulated widely, and the nuisance and political embarrassment of replacing them was one of the restraints that kept countries on a firm commitment to gold. Taking gold coins away, and replacing them by paper or the heavy and inconvenient silver (Shakespeare's "pale and common drudge 'tween man and man"), was unthinkable except in the context of a national catastrophe, as gold embodied progress, prosperity, and propriety. In modern parlance, the sentiment aroused by gold was the system's central commitment mechanism.

The operation of the gold standard occurred on the expectation that it might be suspended in certain circumstances, as in armed conflict between the great powers, but that gold would be restored again at the end of the conflict. The model for this was the British experience of suspending and restoring gold during and after the Napoleonic wars. When the gold standard was restored in the 1920s, however, the experience was destabilizing and unsatisfactory, not simply because it was properly a gold exchange standard, with many countries holding substantial reserves in major currencies such as the dollar and the pound (some countries such as India and Japan in the prewar system had actually held large sterling reserves as a way of economizing on gold). There was also a fundamental difference in that gold coins no longer clinked in citizens' pockets; the cost of an alteration was lower, and thus the possibility of a new departure from gold higher. The 1920s system, unlike the prewar order, did depend on attempts at systematic international rule-making. The critical meeting was the Genoa Monetary Conference of 1922, at which Britain above all laid out the desirability of a generalized return to gold, to be achieved by a substantial degree of international cooperation and harmonization. The recommendations instantly aroused suspicions: did they not very obviously favor British financial interests, and were they not intended to pry open foreign markets for the activities of British banks?

The post–World War II monetary order was also made at a conference, at Bretton Woods. Both the early British and American versions of an agreement provided for a new international unit of account. John Maynard Keynes, who was chiefly responsible for formulating the British position, termed the new unit "bancor" (or "bank gold"). A synthetic currency could be more stable than gold, whose price was subject to arbitrary fluctuations driven not by demand but by the chance of geological exploration and discovery. Keynes was making a bold attempt to wrest the advantages of paper money away from national political control. Privately, however, the chief U.S. negotiator, Harry Dexter White, had always insisted on the preeminent position of the U.S. dollar in the international monetary order, and the conference commission at White's behest inserted a formula according to which countries had to define a "par value" or fixed rate "in terms of gold as a common denominator or in terms of the United States dollar of the weight and fineness in effect on July 1, 1944."[76]

The position of the dollar was immediately controversial, as other countries were at the outset unable to acquire the dollars that they needed for imports, and many commentators began to project that the world would suffer from a permanent and deflationary "dollar shortage." As U.S. capital outflows, as well as military spending abroad, increased in the 1950s and 1960s, the worry turned in the opposite direction, namely that the United States was living beyond its means and imposing its currency on the rest of the world. Since countries had little choice except the dollar as a reserve currency, holdings of dollar reserves increased and made for domestic monetary expansion in the trade partners of the United States. The buildup also caused some nervousness, in that it was theoretically possible that the rest of the world might want to draw on its reserves; and if such a drawing took place abruptly, the result would be a major crisis of confidence.

The person who really moved the debate about the dollar into a discussion of empire was General de Gaulle. In the early 1960s, he complained about how "Western Europe has become, without even being aware of it, a protectorate of the Americans. It is now necessary to free ourselves of this domination. But the difficulty in this case is that the colonies are not really trying to emancipate themselves." The conflicts seemed most immediate to French leaders in the financial and economic area, where France was penetrated by foreign capital. "No domain," the general explained to his assistant Alain Peyrefitte, "escapes from American imperialism. It takes all forms. The most insidious is that of the dollar."[77] In a press conference in February 1964, President de Gaulle memorably termed the position of the United States an "exorbitant privilege." Americans could finance their civilian consumption and their military imperialism with "OPM": Other Peoples' Money. The obsession continued after de Gaulle's departure. The next president of the republic, Georges Pompidou, inserted in hand a passage into Finance Minister Valéry Giscard d'Estaing's 1970 speech to the IMF Annual Meeting to make it clear that the dollar was the root of all evil: "It appears to me that it is necessary, without being aggressive, to show how unhealthy the role of the dollar is and how it is constantly losing its purchasing power. . . . I remember that I said in New York that one could not eternally ask people to set their watches by a defective clock."[78] In the Bretton Woods system, the U.S. financed capital outflows and military expenditures through a buildup of claims on the U.S. dollar. De Gaulle and his successors complained, but they failed to shake the reserve role of the dollar.

When de Gaulle and other critics such as Jean-Jacques Servan-Schreiber originally made their case in the 1960s, they pointed to U.S. trade deficits, but the current account was actually in surplus. The criticism looked much more convincing a few decades later, when the United States built up an apparently structural current account deficit position, and the case that foreign investors and foreign central banks were paying for American consumption became much easier to make.

The dollar remained the central currency of the international order, and the overwhelming share of reserves continued to be held in dollars, even after the collapse of the fixed exchange rate regime in 1971–73. Many commentators, especially in France, at this time wanted to, or thought they could, see a fundamental realignment of the international monetary system away from the dollar. Two French economic writers composed a book on *The Death of the Dollar*, in which they compared the U.S. currency to the worthless paper *assignat* of the French Revolution. They concluded that "the United States, irresponsible banker and corrupt goldsmith, is seriously bankrupt."[79] Serious international attempts at negotiation to find a mechanism or rules under which the U.S. would convert surplus dollars into a basket of currencies (known as the "substitution account") came to nothing. So did ideas, heavily touted in the op-ed sections of the *Wall Street Journal*, the London *Times*, and *Le Monde*, about pushing the world back to a gold standard.

The odd parallelism of the 1960s and the floating-rates era leads those who are suspicious of the United States to spend considerable amounts of time and intellectual energy trying to devise new monetary orders, and institutions that might enable them to pull off something of the American trick. In particular, the long story of European monetary integration is permeated by what economic psychologists might term "dollar envy." Many European currencies—especially the influential case of the Deutschemark—were devised so as to block the political instrumentalization of the hegemonic currency. The demand that currency should limit political choice arose out of consciousness of the need to avoid some of the inflationary problems of the European past. In the aftermath of the two World Wars, European governments that had financed expenditure through the printing press, imposed heavy inflationary traumas on their populations. The Deutschemark carried with it a restrictive vision of what a currency should be, and this concept was transferred to the Euro.

By contrast with the Deutschemark or the Euro, the dollar seemed a "can do" currency, which could be harnessed by its political masters for the national interests of the United States. The more the Europeans were convinced of their own impotence in currency matters, the more they fumed about what they thought was an American master plan to use the dollar for power purposes. The Werner Plan for a European monetary union was drawn up in 1970, as the Bretton Woods system started on its final crisis; the European Monetary System originated in part as a response to the perception that President Jimmy Carter was abusing the world monetary system. The Belgian economist Robert Triffin, who earlier had provided the most compelling critique of the impossible dilemma of the dollar in the Bretton Woods order, described the objectives of the European monetary initiative as the creation of "an oasis of stability less at the mercy of the backwash effects of U.S. policies and policy failures."[80] Proponents of European Monetary Union in the 1990s sometimes (but not always) sounded an anti-American note.

By the 1990s, Europeans criticized the international rescue operations for Mexico in 1994–95 as reflecting preeminently U.S. interests rather than those of the world as a whole. The risk of a Mexican collapse in the absence of massive international assistance did not lie so much in an internationally contagious financial crisis as in a big flow of Mexican workers to their northern neighbor. Similarly in 1997–98, some Europeans joined Asian criticism of the U.S. approach to the Asian financial crisis. They also began to fret about the way in which major commodity prices, especially the politically vital petroleum, were set in dollars, and to demand a more international or less American alternative.

There is a growing tendency, especially where trade, corporate governance, and monetary issues are concerned, to reinterpret the world in power political terms—to see through the imperialism lens rather than that of globalization. This tendency, especially in Europe, marks a deep sense of frustration about the geo-politics and geo-economics of the new post–Cold War era. In the 1960s, the highpoint of the Gaullist attack, Europe could mount not only an intellectual critique, but also a real challenge to the position of the United States and of the dollar. In the early twenty-first century, it cannot, and the real challenges and threats to the stability of the system come from elsewhere. But critics, in large part because they were so powerless, found it easy to resort to using the language of imperialism to describe dollar politics, as well as WTO policy or the new internationalist approach to corporate governance. Consequently, an attack on the arbitrariness of rules came to be a hallmark of the generalized discontent produced by globalization and its uncertainties.

Can It Last?

THE SURVEY in the previous chapter of the rule-based vision of the world economy and its vicissitudes raises the question of how far and long the U.S. role in the system can continue, of the extent to which it depends on the compliance and cooperation of others, and of what sorts of limits are placed on notions of unilateral action. Do states, especially hegemonic states, face a constant danger of overspending their capital and hence of ruin in the manner described by Adam Smith:

> The progress of the enormous debts which at present oppress, and will in the long-run probably ruin, all the great nations of Europe, has been pretty uniform. . . . When national debts have once been accumulated to a certain degree, there is scarce, I believe, a single instance of their having been fairly and completely paid. The liberation of the public revenue, if it has ever been brought about at all, has always been brought about by a bankruptcy; sometimes by an avowed one, but always by a real one, though frequently by a pretended payment.[81]

When countries extrapolate into the future and see some national ruin, they also often think of how rivals will take advantage of any weakness. Discussions of U.S. decline usually assume that there exists a successor, waiting in the wings to take over from the failed hegemon.[82] In the 1980s, the successor was generally held to be Japan or Europe; today the answer is more likely to be India or China (though Europe still has its advocates, who think that Europe is experimenting with a new kind of nontraditional power: see chapter 7). India or China are clearly much farther removed from being able to mount an effective challenge to the major technological, social, or military dimensions of U.S. strength than were the Europeans or the Japanese in the 1980s. In addition, any familiarity with historical precedents would suggest that dynamic and fast growth may lead to greater power, but that on the path to that power there is substantial turbulence and instability.

The United States is unlike conventional historical empires in that its rule depends on cultural and, above all, economic influence rather than territorial domination. Indeed Dominic Lieven pointed out in his wide-ranging survey titled *Empire* that the modern analogues of traditional empires are large ramshackle and inefficiently bureaucratic multi-ethnic states such as India or Indonesia (or even the European Union) rather than the United States.[83] Economic and cultural influence are both, however, characterized by continual mutual interaction that appears to be consensual in a way that imperial military rule is obviously not. Even when critics characterize empires through a simple designation of their respective material products, the results are surprising: while the British Empire was the Maxim gun, American imperialism is supposed to be Coca-Cola or McDonald's.

People buy American products, and especially American services, or American culture, because they need or want them, and because there are no better alternatives. If Americans want to ensure that this form of interaction continues, however, then they need to respond to tastes and demands that change, and their culture will become—as it has indeed been—permeated by the cultures of its markets, clients, and suppliers. An obvious, and widely commented on, phenomenon is the diversification and internationalization of a once famously provincial and monotonous cuisine.

This chapter proposes two ways of thinking about the evolution and development of what was celebrated in the mid-1900s as the "American century." One way is to consider the way in which rules about trade and money interact. The other way involves an examination of the overall position of the United States in the world economy, and the shift away from mid-century large trade surpluses (following from the big productive surge of the U.S. economy in World War II) and large capital exports, to trade deficits and large inflows of capital. This has been an almost evolutionary long-run trend (see figure 3), but it excites particular concern at some critical moments, and dramatic political tensions come to the surface: in the later 1960s, the mid-1980s, and after 2000. Each of these moments of conflict was marked by an interlocking of foreign policy and strategy debates with conflict over economic and

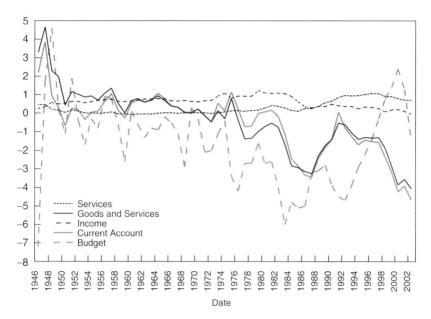

3 U.S. Current Account and Budget Balance, 1946–2002 (share of GDP)

monetary policy: during the Vietnam conflict, the divisions over missile stationing and the Strategic Defense Initiative, and in response to the war on terror and the Iraq conflict.

I

Rules can come in different varieties, and the balance between different rules may shift. The world economy after World War II was rebuilt on the basis of systems of rules and complex institution-building.[84] The rule-building in two critical areas (monetary and trade) moved in opposite directions. During the interwar period, international discussions on international cooperation foundered because trade negotiators believed that while tariff reduction and quota elimination might be desirable, there was no point in discussions until a stable monetary system had been created. Without stable monetary order, the use of restrictive trade measures to stem the export of pernicious deflation could be justified as a desirable second-best measure. On the other hand, the monetary discussions foundered because of reluctance to make agreements while the vicious spiral of trade protection was still underway. During World War II, the United States made it clear that it was not prepared to negotiate on trade liberalization, which it demanded as a prerequisite for a postwar peace, and as a result, all the diplomacy concentrated on a framework of monetary rules (at Bretton Woods). Bretton Woods, of course, created institutions—the World Bank and the IMF—devised to implement the monetary order, but the intended third pillar—the International Trade Organization (ITO)—was left until after the war, and in practice was realized only in the 1990s.

The rule-based monetary order disintegrated in stages between 1968 and 1973. Some consider 1968 as the end of the Bretton Woods regime, in that the collapse of the London gold pool, and the attempt of central banks to maintain a fixed dollar gold price, removed a central reference value of the system; in 1971 the gold parity of the U.S. dollar was reduced, but policymakers tried to find a new set of par values. Only in 1973 did it become clear that such a venture could not command political agreement. After that the IMF's functions changed very dramatically, and it was no longer the legal embodiment of a web of firm commitments about monetary management. Instead its major task turned out to be plugging market failures left by the newly invigorated capital markets: in practice, a great deal of attempt at crisis prevention and a great deal of experience in crisis resolution.

A consensus gradually emerged among U.S. administrations that attempts at international monetary coordination were pointless and counterproductive: like the Bretton Woods order, they restrained monetary policy in a suboptimal way and led to undesired outcomes. Thus the experience of the 1978 Bonn Summit, or the 1985–87 negotiations and semi-agreements about appropriate exchange rates were generally viewed as discrediting the idea of negotiating about exchange rates. The mantra of all U.S. administrations since the 1980s has been that exchange rates are set by the market.

The postwar period produced a great expansion of trade that is fundamental to the story of increased prosperity. Trade became institutionally more regulated. The GATT generalized bilateral agreements, then produced general tariff reductions in the 1960s Kennedy Round, and then became fully institutionalized as the WTO in 1995. Many observers have been surprised by the apparent willingness of the United States to accept rules in this area at each stage of the development of a rule-based order. The story of trade opening can be read as a suspense drama, with a new twist to the narrative on almost every page. The GATT was a compromise. It achieved its biggest successes in the 1960s, largely at the cost of reducing its extent so as to exclude some of the most contentious trade items—textiles and agricultural products. By the 1970s, after the collapse of the Bretton Woods par value system, most writers agreed that the GATT was moribund. The Tokyo Round was protracted and spotty. In the mid-1980s, the leading experts concluded that the GATT was "in a state of breakdown." The ministerial meeting of 1982 had failed. The Uruguay Round looked doomed to failure as the United States and the European Community became locked in a politically complex struggle over agricultural pricing and subsidies. Even in 1993, on the eve of the final agreement of this round, a major text produced by a GATT official had as its theme "the weakening of a multilateral approach to trade relations," "the creeping demise of GATT," and the fact that "the GATT's decline results from the accumulated actions of governments."[85] Then came the astonishing extension of multilateral principles to intellectual property and trade-related investment, as well as the creation of a more complete conflict-resolutions procedure and the institutionalization of multilateralism in the WTO. At that time, the commentators were skeptically insisting that the United States would ignore the new institution and instead continue a unilateral exercise of power through the application of Super 301. When the first ruling came against the United States, however, the country accepted it. In 1998, everyone gave reasons why the financial services agreement could not be realized. Then, what seemed unpredictably, at the last moment it came about. In 2004, the United States made major legal revisions to its trade and tax law to comply with WTO rulings. It ended the Foreign Sales Corporation tax subsidy, which the WTO had determined was illegal; and repealed the 1916 Anti-Dumping Act. Rules still ruled.

In the earlier age of worries about globalization—at the turn of the nineteenth century—a backlash began, which in the end produced restrictions on migration and high levels of trade protection. When national protection became the major priority of most countries, in the 1920s and 1930s, the world became both poorer and less safe. There was a vicious cycle, in which external forces were blamed for loss and disaster, and high levels of trade protection destroyed national prosperity.

Most countries avoided this sort of backlash in the second half of the twentieth century, although their citizens had the same angst. There are obvious parallels between British concerns about German competition, on the basis of cheap labor in the 1880s and 1890s, and worries of Americans about the Japanese threat in the 1960s and 1970s and that of China today. The changing of employment patterns is a constant accompaniment of growth and transformation in the economy, and trade rather than technology tends to be blamed for the bad labor market consequences. In the early 1970s and again in the 1980s U.S. workers and producers were upset about the loss of jobs to Japan. Some of the most skilled jobs, in automobiles, were lost; household appliances like TVs were no longer made in the United States. On each occasion, the administration tried to respond to the job loss worries not by imposing trade restrictions but by altering exchange rates to make the U.S. products more competitive: first by ending the gold convertibility of the dollar in 1971, and then in 1985 by negotiating the Plaza Agreement to depreciate the dollar. Monetary and exchange rate policy initiatives offered a way of absorbing adjustment pain. The focus of trade discontent was shifted to the monetary arena in a way that helped to undermine the legitimacy of institutional ways of regulating the international financial system.

The use of monetary policy and exchange rate adjustment to deescalate trade conflict is harder today, since many of the countries whose products are entering the United States peg their own currencies to the dollar. Governments still feel that they need some response in an attempt to "feel the pain," and to show that they are doing something. Like the George W. Bush administration they adopt tariffs (such as that levied on steel imports in 2002) that may then be overruled by the WTO. In this way they do nothing very harmful, but point out to the electorate that their hands are tied by international agreements and institutions. But this sort of action itself then produces a new kind of backlash, against the international institutions.

Trade problems are in fact routinely dealt with by shifting the emphasis to the monetary arena. The world has developed its institutional arrangements in the setting of globalization by making them harder in the trade arena and softer in the monetary one. In the future the off-loading of adjustment problems to monetary policy will be more difficult because of widespread Asian exchange rate pegging and because of the new informal and largely privatized character of the international monetary system. Something of this reverse reaction is evident in the Schumer-Graham Amendment passed by the U.S. Senate in 2005, which placed a 27.5 percent tariff on all Chinese goods entering the United States unless China revalued its currency. Monetary issues now produce trade responses. The lesson is clear: the world trading system will consequently be more vulnerable.

II

Can the post–Bretton Woods order blow up in a manner analogous to that of the disintegration of Bretton Woods? This is the fundamental fear of those who think that U.S. current account deficits are unsustainable, and are worried about the way in which the United States attracts over an amazing three quarters of net international capital inflows (75.5 percent in 2002).[86] There is an obvious contrast with British imperial experience, and the resilience of the British Empire owed a great deal to its long-term current account surplus position from the mid-nineteenth century to World War I. By contrast, Imperial Spain in its Golden Era in the sixteenth and seventeenth centuries had permanent deficits, financed by the extraction of precious metals. It deindustrialized and lost the basis for preeminence. Is the United States more Spanish than British?

The current account position of the United States reflects a long-term shift. In 1946, the current account surplus was 3.9 percent of GDP, with a merchandise trade balance of +$6,697 million and a (nonmilitary) services balance of +$1,043 million. The United States had built up a substantial creditor position in the world economy, which became even bigger over the course of the next thirty years as American corporations pumped investment all over the world, and transformed the local economies of Western Europe and Japan. Net investment income in 1946 amounted to $560 million. By 1971, when the international monetary system built around the fixed exchange rate (Bretton Woods) regime collapsed, the current account had shrunk to a small deficit, equivalent to 0.1 percent of GNP, and there was a negative merchandise balance (−$2,260 million), a small surplus on services, and very substantial earnings from the investment assets built up overseas during the previous twenty years ($7,272 million). In 1985, when tight monetary policies combined with a big fiscal deficit sent the dollar to a spiky peak, there was a large current account deficit of $118,155 million, or 2.8 percent of GDP, and a surge in earnings from investment ($25,723 million). At this point, the United States became a net debtor, and a major recipient of foreign inflows, but the earnings on investment remained very high through the 1990s, as the U.S. debtor position became ever more extreme.

There are two complementary ways of thinking about the balance of payments as it developed since the 1980s, and hence of judging its sustainability. The first is that it is a reflection of the relative attraction of foreign assets for U.S. residents and of U.S. assets for those outside. The deficit is driven by the high demand for U.S. assets, and its sustainability depends on the continuance of this demand. Through much of the 1990s, it was primarily private-sector flows that accounted for the inflows, on the basis of a calculation that high rates of productivity growth were creating a peculiarly American economic miracle. But in economics, miracles are rare. In fact, the identification of a phenomenon as a miracle is usually an indication that there is some speculative bubble that is about to burst.

Since 2000, and the collapse of the dot.com bubble, those private flows have been replaced by central bank purchases, largely by dynamic and rapidly growing Asian countries, and especially by China. The motivation is a desire to hold Asian exporters' exchange rates down, and thus build jobs in an export sector as migrants flock into glittering coastal cities from an impoverished inland and a low-productivity rural sector. It is also a response to the monetary problems caused by large inflows of Foreign Direct Investment (FDI), which partly fuels and partly responds to the phenomenon of strong growth and innovation; as well as by speculative "hot money" or short-term inflows aimed at deriving a quick gain from an imminent revaluation of the currency. This strategy looks like a replay of the technique used by Western Europe and

Japan to pull themselves out of their mid-century collapse in the aftermath of fascism and war. They too used undervalued currencies to ensure that wages remained internationally competitive and thus to fuel an export offensive.[87]

It is possible to see this recent, early-twenty-first century, twist as a pact between an Asia trading bloc and the United States to let low-cost Asian exports flow to the American consumer, in which both sides benefit and the costs are largely imposed on a third party. The European economies, with a flexible exchange rate against the dollar, and inflexible domestic markets, see their relative costs rise as the dollar depreciates relative to the Euro and the other European currencies. The Asian-American tango might be strained, not by anything the Europeans can do, but because of the possible responses of the two partners. Both sides have strong incentives to let the relationship continue, but at the same time they are both deeply anxious about an inherent fragility.

The Asian side looks vulnerable to inflationary risks, as it is practically impossible to sterilize the large inflows of dollars. The result is that the massive dollar surges prompt asset price bubbles, especially in real estate, in the same way as the big capital flows of the mid-1990s did in the case of Korea or Thailand. Some commentators, notably Barry Eichengreen, make the point that this presents a major contrast with the Western European and Japanese experience of the 1960s, where the dollar inflows were largely directed to productive investments and the building up of infrastructure as multinational enterprises brought in a transformative business culture.[88] Even in the 1960s, in the last phases of the Bretton Woods system, the Europeans began to complain about the inflation that U.S. policies were allegedly imposing on them, and labor radicalism broke the postwar bargain that had been at the center of the export boom. The Asian central banks may also be increasingly worried about the extent of losses on their dollar reserves in the aftermath of a possible depreciation of the dollar.[89] But it is hard to see what they might reasonably do to avoid such losses, as any attempt to diversify their assets would almost certainly lead to a dollar sell-off and thus a confirmation of the extent of their loss. The implication of the historical lesson is that a modern version of the Bretton Woods compromise, between Asia and the United States, is much more likely to be short-lived than was the

1960s variant, which did not survive that long either. Even as long as it lasts, the participants are bound to see the fragility and how it generates constant nervousness in the markets.

From the other side, the United States has little motive to disrupt a mechanism from which its citizens have gained substantially. The risk is rather that a massive loss of confidence would lead to a shift in reserve assets away from the U.S. dollar. Unlike in the 1960s, when there was no alternative currency that could be used as a reserve base, in the millennium world the Euro offers such an opportunity, and Asian governments are actively trying to promote an Asian currency–based bond market. It is paradoxical that worries about the bilateral trade deficit with China lead to political pressure on China for an upward revaluation of the renminbi exchange rate, an action that would be very likely to lead to an unraveling of the new monetary order.

One apparently odd fact makes the deficits more sustainable than most analysts believed they should be: the yield on U.S. assets for foreigners—the price paid by the United States for its borrowing—is substantially lower than the yield for Americans on their foreign holdings. This is the reason why the balance on investment income continues to be so surprisingly resilient and large.[90] The yield difference reflects not miscalculation or stupidity on the part of foreign investors, but a calculation in which they buy security in return for lower yields. The primary attraction of the United States as a destination for capital movement is the unique depth of its markets (which generate a financial security) and the political and security position of the country. This is why inflows to the United States may increase after global security shocks (as they did after September 11). Such a conclusion emphasizes the extent to which the world monetary order is driven more and more by political considerations.

The ability of the United States to finance its deficits therefore depends on the continued perception that it is a high-growth and high-productivity economy and that it is politically and militarily secure. Conversely, the security of the United States depends on the continued inflow of capital, as a sudden adjustment would be unbearably painful and intolerable politically.

The painfulness of adjustment will become apparent in considering the other way of thinking about the U.S. balance of payments position:

a relationship between saving and investment in the United States. As long as investment is high and saving is low, the gap is financed from abroad. Low levels of saving reflect a high commitment to consumption. Contrary to popular belief particularly outside the United States, this is not fundamentally the result of an addiction to outrageous forms of conspicuous consumption such as SUVs.[91] (Though there are some odd statistics that seem to bear parts of this thesis out: Americans spend more on jewelry today than on shoes.)[92] Yet expenditure on food and clothing as a proportion of income has fallen quite dramatically over recent decades, expenditure on housing remains more or less constant, and the big growth has been in spending on education and health. Many academic economists (who have an obvious interest as educators) would like to reclassify these as forms of investment in human capital, and it is probably true that the continued innovative capacity of the United States depends on quality education. We can also get much or at least some benefit by attracting highly educated people from other parts of the world; and the export of people trained in American universities is a vital part of Joseph Nye's idea of "soft power."[93]

Another element of the over-consumption theory arises out of the contemplation of the link between fiscal issues and the current account. Government spending on the military is a form of consumption. During the Vietnam era, the Reagan defense buildup, and in the post-2001 years, military spending was a current issue in international discussions of the stability of the monetary and financial order. In all these cases, increased defense expenditure went hand in hand with domestically oriented fiscal expansion—for example, to create the Great Society, or for Reagan and George W. Bush to cut taxes. It is as if the United States could not gather the domestic support for defense or war without buying social content at home. De Gaulle's criticism of the United States seems a peculiarly timeless expression of how Europeans view each of these incidents: "The United States is not capable of balancing its budget. It allows itself to have enormous debts. Since the dollar is the reference currency everywhere, it can cause others to suffer the effects of its poor management. This is not acceptable. This cannot last."[94]

The "cannot last" issue is, however, the one that raises the link between the capacity to borrow and its dependence on continued economic dynamism. In the late-nineteenth-century era of open capital markets, inflows to high-growth countries (such as the United States or Australia) were sustained over very long periods of time.

The question about sustainability then turns into one about the probability of continued growth rates that are higher than those of the rest of the industrialized world. For much of the 1990s, foreign capital inflows reflected a foreign view that the peace dividend, fiscal prudence, and technological dynamism represented an ideal environment. In the years after 2001, this environment clearly deteriorated.

Growth rates are threatened by long-term fiscal problems arising both out of military commitments and the burdens of ensuring social security for an aging population: in this respect the United States shares (in a less extreme form) a problem that is also emerging in the aging in-dustrial societies of Europe and Japan.[95] The deterioration of the fiscal position in the beginning of the millennium was a general and transna-tional phenomenon: the average general government fiscal balance for all the advanced industrial economies in 2000 was exactly in balance, while in 2004 the figure had slid to a deficit of 3.9 percent. The U.S. po-sition, with a change from a 1.3 percent surplus (2000) to −4.9 percent, looks like an extreme example of the transformation, but Germany moved from 1.3 percent to −3.9 percent, France from −1.4 to −3.4, and Italy from −0.6 to −2.9, while Japan stayed with very high deficit levels showing only a slight improvement (−7.5 changing to −6.9).[96] Fiscal problems thus pose a long-term threat to the capacity of the United States to sustain growth and hence capital inflows (although the United States is by no means alone in its fiscal predicament).

The world economic environment is however clearly not made by the United States alone. The likelihood of bad effects coming from crises elsewhere is increased by increased financial turbulence and also by the deinstitutionalization of international monetary relations as dis-cussed earlier. To go back to the immediate post-1945 vision, Bretton Woods aimed at establishing an institution (the IMF) to manage re-serves. Now reserve positions held at the IMF play a minor role, and the major holders of reserves are national central banks, as they were before World War II.

On the other hand, explosive and contagious debt crises in the past have been in part reflections of the policy mix in advanced industrial countries. In the early 1980s, or mid-1990s, high interest rates worldwide changed the debt dynamics and made previously tolerable levels of debt unsustainable and thus touched off creditor panics. In the modern scenario, the effects of expansive fiscal policies, not just in the United States but also in many European countries, will in the longer term be likely to result in real interest rate rises.

In this setting, the buildup of large claims on the United States—especially in the form of the massive reserve holdings of Asian central banks—is a potential danger. Asian reserves in early 2004 accounted for over two-thirds of the world's reserves, and Japan holds some $650 billion in U.S. (mostly Treasury) securities and China $420 billion. As the inflows of funds into Asia continued, by 2005 the major Asian central banks held $1,800 billion in dollar reserves (out of a total reserve holding of some $2,400 billion). Of the U.S. government debt, 37.3 percent was held abroad in 2004, compared with 4.7 percent in 1965 when General de Gaulle believed that he needed to criticize U.S. dollar politics. The danger today probably lies less in the political instrumentalization of these reserves (such as would be represented by a de Gaulle–like conversion of dollars into something else, probably Euros). There might be a certain political attraction of such an anti-American action at particular moments, but it would be enormously costly for those who undertake it since it would push down the value of the dollar assets very quickly and substantially. The risk is that these reserves are unlikely to be held perpetually for economic rather than political reasons. The world of liberalized capital movements that evolved in the 1990s has seen remarkable shifts and reversals of direction of capital flows. So the question arises what if Japan, or more probably China or (even more probably) India (which has also been recently accumulating reserves very rapidly), needs to use them?

This is an area where the costs of the deinstitutionalization of the international monetary system may become apparent. In the 1990s, contagious financial crises were handled by big IMF-coordinated rescue operations. The big capital account crises of the 1990s involved much larger amounts of support relative to previous crises. Mexico in 1995 drew 688 percent of its quota; Korea in 1997–98, 1939 percent; Argentina in 2001, 800 percent, and Turkey in 2002 1330 percent. Before the 1990s, there had been an inclination to give too little in the way of incentives for program countries to make adjustment and reforms.

When the emphasis shifted to reassuring nervous markets in a capital account crisis, the priorities were reversed, and stabilizing the expectations of the markets would involve the assurance of so much support that speculators could not take a position against a country or currency and hope to succeed. This function had an analogy to the role of central banks in national economies as lenders of last resort, an analogy that was controversially drawn by the IMF's First Managing Director Stanley Fischer.[97] The parallel is sometime made to the Colin Powell doctrine about military intervention: that it only makes sense if conducted with massive and overwhelming force.

The aftermath of the big bailouts in the 1990s is acutely controversial. The immediate criticism, which was probably overstated, was that it produced a moral hazard problem. In the view of Milton Friedman, for instance, the 1995 Mexican program produced the Asian crisis of 1997 because investors assumed a Fund guarantee. This may have played some part in investors' calculations, but they were fundamentally impressed by the idea of an "East Asian miracle" that they should buy into. There is an analogy with the development of the stock market boom in industrial countries in the late 1990s: some of it may have been driven by the idea that central banks (and in particular the Federal Reserve) would support a certain level of the market, but mostly it was driven by a vision of a "New Economy."

The real problems came from the size of the rescue operations, the strain that these caused for the IMF's resources, and the fact that as a result such operations could not be envisaged for a large number of countries simultaneously. This increasingly obvious limitation brought an element of intellectual incoherence to the whole approach, which was particularly visible in the stance of the United States. Paul O'Neill, as treasury secretary in the Bush administration, repeatedly attacked the idea of "big bailouts" in principle, but then went on to advocate them very forcefully in particular cases, often in the face of resistance from other G-7 countries that wanted to interpret them as political opportunism.

There is a likelihood that as India and China continue to grow and move toward the liberalization of the capital account, there will be repeats of the abrupt reversals of capital movements that afflicted many or indeed most emerging markets. The same cycle of inflows, speculative domestic bubbles, over-investment, and a rapid collapse of confidence that characterized the dynamic Asian economies of the "Asian miracle" in the 1990s is likely to be repeated. High growth is usually—as it was in the nineteenth-century United States, or in Korea since the 1960s—quite uneven and prone to sudden setbacks and crises of confidence. But the scale of potential reversals in India or China are so much greater than anything that the world dealt with in the 1990s, that it is likely that the world financial system will become more vulnerable than at any time since 1945. The United States will be unable to isolate itself from this general financial volatility. Historically, eras of financial volatility have tended to tip the balance against globalization.

The Victory of Mars

The "GLOBALIZATION" view is not always popular, and it seems to be subject to pendulum swings and backlashes. Some of the backlash stems from the political and social psychology inherent in globalization, and in particular in the resentments brought by changes in relative income and wealth. Gibbon concluded, "Such is the constitution of civil society, that, whilst a few persons are distinguished by riches, by honours, and by knowledge, the body of the people is condemned to obscurity, ignorance, and poverty."[98] Inequality was the social problem that provoked the rise of what he saw as the ideology that would undermine the Roman empire.

By the end of the twentieth century, ancient Rome looked much farther away than it did for eighteenth-century British analysts. This is because the late twentieth century largely saw the victory of the globalizers. With this triumph came an immense self-satisfaction and complacency about the inherent strength and resilience of the system. The sort of analysis that was given by Joseph Schumpeter began to look very dated.[99] From the perspective of the middle of the twentieth century, he had offered on the one hand a celebration of the creative achievements of a liberal capitalistic world order, but on the other, the prognosis that the resentments generated would bring down the system. Anti-globalization protest in the 1990s, while widespread, was—as even its most militant enthusiasts recognized—intellectually incoherent and diffuse. The more rational anti-globalization figures insisted that they wanted a better or more just globalization, a unification of people rather than of capitalistic interests. Both the pro-globalizers and the anti-globalizers were overconfident about the stability of the globally integrated economy.

One of the comfort blankets that modern people clutch is the idea that there was only ever one big simultaneous world depression, produced by such an odd confluence of causes as to be quite unique: the legacy of World War I and of the financial settlement of reparations and war debt; the chaotic banking system of the largest economy of the world, the United States; and inexperience in handling monetary policy in a world that was still pining for metallic money. Since these circumstances were so unique, they can't occur again. Historians should say that this reasoning might be quite wrong.

A great deal of the historically informed literature on globalization makes the point that there were several previous eras of increased worldwide integration that came to a halt, and were reversed, with painful consequences. The most familiar precedent for modern globalization is that of the late nineteenth and early twentieth century, which ended definitively with the interwar Great Depression. There were also earlier epochs of integration: the Roman empire, the economic rebound of the late fifteenth and early sixteenth centuries (the economic backdrop to the Renaissance), or the eighteenth century, in which improved technology and increased ease of communications opened the way to global empires (for Britain and France).

All of these previous globalization episodes ended, almost always with wars. Bad policies can obviously wreck individual economies in a whole range of different ways; but systemic collapse is a product of militarized conflict. Globalization as an economic phenomenon depends on the movement across state boundaries of goods, labor, and capital. Security concerns produce heightened worries about all these kinds of mobility. Trade may create a dependence on imports that leads to strategic vulnerability, and one of the oldest arguments for agricultural protection was the need for autarkic self-sufficiency in case of attack. Labor flows may camouflage the movement of spies or saboteurs. Thus, for instance, World War I Britain was gripped by panic about the numbers of Germans employed in London restaurants. Finally, capital controls have often been justified on grounds of national security. One way of destabilizing politics was to try to promote financial panic, and restrictions on capital mobility might be a way of generating increased immunity to speculative attack.

There are obvious analogies in some of these past experiences to some of the threats to the economic order and to economic integration posed by the war on terror. Trade, financial flows, and labor movements are all vulnerable in the post–September 11 world. After September 11, every part of the package that had previously produced such unprecedented economic growth in many countries—the increased flow of people, goods, and capital—now seem to contain obvious threats to security. Students and visitors from poor and especially from Islamic countries might be "sleeper" terrorists; or they might become radicalized through their experience of Western liberalism, permissiveness, or the arbitrariness of the market economy. It soon became apparent that customs agencies scarcely controlled the shipment of goods any longer, and that explosives, or even ABC (atomic, biological, chemical) weapons might easily be smuggled. The free flow of capital, and complex bank transactions, might be used to launder money and to supply funding for terrorist operations.

It is natural and legitimate to suggest that all these areas should be subject to more intense controls in the face of security threats. Yet there is a danger of giving an absolute priority to the war against terrorism. Every sort of control also offers a possibility for abuse by people who want controls for other reasons: because skilled immigrant workers provide "unfair" competition; because too many goods are imported from cheap labor countries; or because capital movements are believed to be destabilizing, producing severe and contagious financial crises. A new debate about the security challenge offered the chance to present older demands for the protection of particular interests in a much more dramatic and compelling way. Protectionists of all sorts suddenly had a good story to tell about the harm done by international trade.

Is this the recurrent collapse of globalization and the phenomenon of war an accidental or coincidental linkage?

There are two major ways in which war undermines globalization. The first, most obvious (and the one that has been most studied), is simply the consequence of the cost of war considered in a broad sense: the problem of financing unproductive military activity, the disruption of commerce, the suspension of migration, and the freezing of capital movements because of security priorities. The second is the way in which armed conflict, even when its scope is quite small, provokes the emergence of new issues that produce international discord that then affects other areas of international interaction. In this way, war challenges assumptions about the global distribution of economic and political power.

The idea that war is costly and disrupts "normal commerce" is well understood in the classic literature of economics. Indeed, for those who experienced the wars of the American and French revolutions, how could it be otherwise? Adam Smith's first volume of the *Wealth of Nations* (1776) closes at the end of Book III with the reflection that "the ordinary revolutions of war and government easily dry up the sources of that wealth which arises from commerce alone."[100] Such disruption arises most immediately and most obviously in the case of sustained and major conflict.

Most periods of modern conflict have been accompanied by inflationary war finance and followed by sharp periods of deflation. The most obvious mechanism that made for postwar deflation is the effect of increased government expenditure on interest rates. An alternative way of thinking about this is to consider it as the destruction or wearing out of capital in wartime, which makes for a higher price of new capital. The rise in real long-term interest rates makes peacetime investment more expensive and depresses activity. This effect is enhanced if governments try to return to prewar exchange rate systems with prices and wages that have been boosted and distorted by the high levels of wartime demand.

Almost all of the most dramatic historical episodes of sustained deflation followed in the aftermath of war. A sustained economic depression followed the American War of Independence, and accentuated the initial anticommercial bias of the politics of the new Republic. After the Congress of Vienna (1814–15) ended the Napoleonic wars, Europe had decades of deflation, in which industrial investment was costly and the bankruptcy of entrepreneurs frequent. The aftermath of the 1860s civil wars (or wars of unification) in Italy, Germany, and the United States all included an immediate speculative bubble, and then the bursting of the bubble (after 1873), with stock market price collapses, bankruptcies, and reduced investment. World War I was also followed by a brief reconstruction boom in 1919, and then by a collapse in the major Western economies in 1920–21; one decade later came the Great Depression.[101] Some of these classic effects in which war produces monetary instability are still very visible in the aftermath of the major international

conflicts of the post-1945 era. Korea and Vietnam both produced inflationary surges, which initially reduced and then increased real interest
rates, and which corresponded to investment surges and declines.

The 1991 Gulf War no longer fits this pattern: both inflation and interest rates fell. It was followed by a brief recession, which is generally
held by political analysts to have frustrated the reelection of President
George H. W. Bush in the 1992 election. The 1990s war was simply too
small-scale and cheap to have a major macroeconomic impact: and this
holds true for 2003 too. If there is a threat, it arises out of long term developments in domestic spending which are characteristic of almost all
industrial societies (see above).

One explanation of the changing effects of war in very recent times is
obvious: the cost of each war for the major superpower has been falling
since the middle of the twentieth century. In 2002 dollars, World War II
cost the United States $4,700 billion, Korea $400 billion, Vietnam $572
billion, the 1991 Gulf War $80 billion, and the actual fighting in the
Iraq war of 2003 cost little over $20 billion.[102] It would consequently be
appropriate to expect a diminution of the purely fiscal impact of wars,
and consequently of their deflationary legacy.

If we simply take a naïve approach to the demand and supply for
military action, falling costs should suggest increased demand and a
new likelihood of the use of force to effect regime change. The less a
war costs, and the fewer the casualties, both military and civilian, the
more likely it becomes. The declining willingness of advanced industrial societies to use force in the second half of the twentieth century,
which has been noted by many observers from Edward Luttwak to Jeremy Black,[103] and which is sometimes attributed to the much larger
political impact of casualty figures, is thus not likely to be a permanent
phenomenon. Countries such as France, Britain, and the United States
actually showed a surprising willingness to sustain casualties, and to respond to calls for the need to maintain order in remote parts of the
world. As long as there is a clear technical military superiority, cases for
a morally and politically appropriate use of force will continue to be
quite powerful.

Adam Smith made a similar point about some of the wars of the
eighteenth century. The combination of technology, which made war
between advanced and backward countries less costly for the advanced

country, and new methods of spreading the financial burden of war through the sale of debt instruments, was making war more likely. "In great empires the people who live in the capital, and in the provinces remote from the scene of action, feel, many of them, scarce any inconveniency from the war; but enjoy, at their ease, the amusement of reading in the newspapers the exploits of their own fleets and armies."[104]

The same conclusion can be reached by a less cynical route. During the Cold War and the period of superpower tensions, wars were held in check by a widespread realization that the cost of their escalation would be too high. Since the end of the Cold War, however, there has been a proliferation of international as well as of threatening domestic conflicts as states break up. Hence the need for intervention.

Some commentators have already jumped to the conclusion that it is wrong simply to think about the cost of military conflict, and that in particular the growing expense and political embarrassment of post-conflict Iraq precludes another such conflict. This reasoning is fallacious, because similar situations are highly likely to recur. We are internationally sensitive to human rights issues, and also to the potential of bad governments to destabilize whole regions. Both concerns are realistic, and, I would add, creditable. They will necessarily lead to military engagements in sometimes expected and sometimes unexpected places. Moreover, it is possible to envisage more attention being paid in advance to the management of post-conflict situations in a manner that in the Iraq case was made impossible by the rush of events.

Wars also lead to questions about the legitimacy of rules that are essential in guiding economic interaction, both internationally and also domestically. All wars, big or small, produce new problems and divisions. There has been a spillover from security concerns to economics. The most obvious type arises out of the financial legacies of wars and debates about reparations and war debts. Such debates poisoned the international economy in the 1920s (as Keynes predicted in *The Economic Consequences of the Peace*). They are presently recurring in the fierce debate about whether and how and what kind of prewar Saddam debt should be forgiven to help Iraq in reconstruction.

One tradition of thinking about wars (and especially of the smaller scale wars of the classical late-nineteenth-century era of globalization) suggests that they have economic origins, and that they are fought—especially in eras of globalization—because of a wish to control a greater share of global resources. This is familiar to historians and social scientists as the Hobson-Hilferding-Lenin interpretation of imperialism.[105] It is largely wrong as an explanation of the origins of wars, but at the same time it is very powerful in understanding the political response to them.

This paradox arises because of other effects of eras of globalization. New opportunities to create new wealth mean radical changes in distributions. Big corporations became powerful. Large and apparently illegitimate increases in fortune provoke resentments and a populist reaction. There are clear historical precedents to the current worldwide wave of reaction against and rejection of what is now perceived as U.S.-style capitalism.

Martin Luther's protest against the universalism of the Renaissance world took the form of a protest against the "luxury" of long-distance and foreign trade:

> But foreign trade, which brings from Calcutta and India and such places wares like costly silks, articles of gold and spices—which minister only to ostentation but serve no useful purpose, and which drain away the money of land and people—would not be permitted if we had proper government and princes.[106]

The eighteenth century, in which both the French and the British East India companies unfolded their activities to the full, spanning continents, qualifies by most measures as an era of globalization. The protests that the East India Companies excited, because of their global reach, and because of their use of low-wage labor for some part of their production, have a very modern tone. Adam Smith showed how the activities of the East India Company in Bengal had reduced incomes and induced widespread famine.[107] Here were unaccountable companies, distributing luxury products that were unnecessary and that were believed by many Christian ministers to be morally pernicious. Smith concluded, "Such exclusive companies . . . are nuisances in every respect; always more or less inconvenient to the countries in which they are established, and destructive to those which have the misfortune to fall under their government."[108] The history of the United States began with an anti-globalization revolt directed against a particular company, not the British monarchy: the dumping of tea in Boston harbor was a protest not just against taxes but against the business practices of the East India Company.

In the mother country, the outcry over the East India Company focused increasingly on what was then called "exorbitance": the disproportionate remuneration of corporate executives. Warren Hastings, the Governor General, was eventually impeached in public trial by the British parliament. In 1777 his pay had been £10,000, but he had sent home precisely this amount, and in 1778 he sent £45,000 back home to England.[109]

The same sort of debates were repeated in the globalization phase of the late nineteenth century, when they were linked with a critique of imperialist war. The British liberal J. A. Hobson, and the Marxists who adapted his explanation as a vital new stage in their historical model of development, had in mind not the totally destructive conflict of twentieth-century war but rather the relatively short, nontotal, war that characterized the era of high globalization. The Spanish-American War (1898) brought the United States into the international system. It was, unlike the sustained conflicts earlier in the nineteenth century, a very unequal conflict between the world's fastest growing and largest industrial economy, and a very backward European imperial power. The United States deployed 274,000 soldiers, but only 379 were killed. It was soon followed by another unequal conflict, the British conquest of the Boers.

Hobson elaborated his theory of imperialism first as a journalistic interpretation of the British action in South Africa. His reports from South Africa for the *Manchester Guardian* were published when he came back to England as *The War in South Africa*, an attack on the financial elite that wanted to exploit the diamond monopoly and thus had overthrown the government of the Transvaal. He began his most famous work with an explanation of the reasons why modern imperialism was much more unstable than that of the ancient Romans. It was an outgrowth of nationalism in a world of competing states, while Roman imperialism "contained a genuine element of internationalism." "The root idea of empire in the ancient and medieval world was that of a federation of States, under a hegemony, covering in general terms the entire known recognized world, such as was held by Rome under the so-called *pax romana*."[110]

Hobson was also very careful to distinguish imperialism from the settlement of colonists in more-or-less uninhabited parts of the world. Modern imperialism was commercially useless, in that it added to the empire "tropical and sub-tropical regions with which our trade is small, precarious and unprogressive." Imperialism, unlike settler colonialism, made "for greater complications of foreign policy, greater centralisation of power, and a congestion of business which ever threatens to absorb and overtax the capacity of parliamentary government." Cliques of businessmen were spending public resources, "the blood and money of the people in this vast and disastrous military game, feigning national antagonisms which have no basis in reality." "The South African war, openly fomented by gold speculators for their private purposes, will rank in history as a leading case of this usurpation of nationalism." Individuals used the principle of property rights, which they extended across national frontiers, to call on their state to back up their own financial interests, irrespective of whether this was for any general good. Transnational capitalism resulted from "the growing stake of our wealthy classes in countries over which they have no political control."[111]

Both unequal wars, the Spanish-American and the Boer conflict, were acutely controversial in domestic politics and could be interpreted as "land grabs," demands for resources that were scarce: sugar from the Caribbean, and diamonds (from the Kimberley field) and gold in southern Africa. At first the wars produced electorally successful nationalism, with the 1900 British "khaki election" turning out a large Conservative and imperialist vote, and a surge of popularity for Theodore Roosevelt, who had been the hero of the 1898 war. Then there was a backlash, in which critics pointed out associations between war and personal gains of a small group of corrupt businessmen and financiers.

In Britain, Leo Chiozza Money denounced the corruption of finance. Hobson was quite explicit about the villain, "speculation":

a word whose meaning becomes more sinister when politics and private business are so inextricably interwoven as they were in the career of Mr. [Cecil] Rhodes, who used the legislature of the Cape Colony to support and strengthen the diamond monopoly of De Beers, while from De Beers he financed the Raid, debauched the constituencies of Cape Colony, and bought the public press, in order to engineer the war, which was to win him full possession of his great 'thought' the North.

The imperialists operated by means of propaganda, a trick of the "incitation and direction of the brute lusts of human domination which are everywhere latent in civilized humanity, for the pursuance of a policy fraught with material gain to a minority of co-operative vested interests which usurp the title of the commonwealth."[112] The Liberals made much of the hypocrisy of the British government, which denounced the racial discrimination of the Boers while under the Labour Ordinance of 1904 it encouraged a massive Chinese immigration to provide labor for the development of southern Africa. They won a stunning electoral victory in 1906. An anti-imperialist reaction also arose in the United States, where the mood turned against the financiers who had bought the election of President McKinley in 1896. Roosevelt himself began to denounce "certain malefactors of great wealth" who had appropriated many of the gains produced by public action. Populists presented war and corporate scandal as going hand in hand.

These wars also made international relations significantly more tense. The Boer War was one of the quite decisive moments in the growing breach between Britain and Germany, with the German kaiser publicly supporting the Boers. This case illustrates how small conflicts set the stage for bigger and more global clashes, in which arguments over the distribution of spoils worsen the international climate. They also feed a mood which tends to interpret commercial conflict—such as that between Britain and Germany in the later years of the nineteenth century, or between Japan and the United States in the late twentieth century, or between China and the United States in the early twenty-first century—as inherently political and strategic as well as economic. The recent episodes produced as a consequence a way of forecasting "coming wars," such as *The Coming War with Japan*.[113]

At these moments, the different sides begin to see the way they do business in a contrasting way, which is quite at odds with the "one world" approach of the "globalization paradigm." To stay with the pre–World War I example, prominent Germans began to attack the hypocritical "commercialism" of the British hegemon. They depicted themselves as the bearer of a more heroic and more noble sort of society, in which "heroes" rather than "traders" set the tone. Those who developed this distinction, notably the economist Werner Sombart, went on to argue that German businessmen too shared in this heroic quality, because they went about business in a different way and would sacrifice short-term profit for long-term communal and national interest.[114] The images of the virtues of different national forms of capitalism created by Sombart live on, a century later, as the contrast between a caring relationship-based long-term vision of continental European capitalism and a short-term speculative and rapacious "Anglo-Saxon capitalism."

To make business conform more to a supposedly superior national model, more control is needed. The wish to see a particular model of capitalism, aligned with a particular social vision, produces massive and disruptive social pathologies. In the background of the old-style European condemnation of speculative capitalism often lay anti-Semitic stereotypes. There are obvious parallels in recent times to the way in which reactions against the apparent unfairness of market capitalism target ethnic or religious minorities who are held to have positions of unfair or undue influence. Amy Chua has recently produced a bestseller documenting the backlashes against what she calls "market dominant ethno-national minorities": Chinese in much of Asia, Indians in southern Africa, Lebanese in West Africa, Jews in former Soviet Republics.[115] In none of these cases is it likely that attacks on the minority, including looting and despoliation, will lead to anything except poverty and disruption. Violent ethno-nationalism is a powerful and highly economically disruptive force, and is characteristic of periods of reaction against the globalization paradigm.

In such protest, the enemy is targeted as rich, international, or transnational, and is linked to some kind of imperialism. The political tensions of the modern globalization phase go hand in hand with a revived discussion of contrasting national models of capitalism, and a new degree of skepticism about the "Anglo-Saxon model." This new mood can be linked to wider economic and political concerns.

In Asia, a higher level of trust is ascribed to complex enterprises and networks of enterprises held together by close friendship and kinship ties. A greater degree of trust allowed the elaboration of long-term plans, whose benefits did not simply accrue with each immediate trans-action. This style of business was celebrated in the early 1990s as largely responsible for an "Asian miracle," and then was vilified in 1997–98 by "Western" economists as "crony capitalism." It then became attractive again, and blended with traditional and long-existing anti-Western ste-reotypes. Continental Europeans also wanted to defend a long-term, stakeholder, model of capitalism.

In part the new European sensibility is the product of anxiety about the viability of small firms in an era of global competition. In part too, Europeans are naturally worried about the dismantling of the welfare state, and about the costs of their aging population and the conse-quences of their low birth rates. This debate produces defensive images of an order that needs to be protected, as well as yielding hostile visions of the outside world and its ethos. Enron has become a rallying cry of the anti-globalization movement. Business figures in Europe who had once tried to present themselves as advocates of an American-style capitalism or of "shareholder value" such as Thomas Middelhoff or Ron Sommer or Jean-Marie Messier were now excoriated as incompetent or corrupt (which in many cases, needless to say, they had been). European execu-tives were put on trial for agreeing to supposedly excessive compensation packages.

It is important to note that the attempts to formulate new visions of nationally distinctive and anti-global capitalisms are not just a product of anti-American reactions to perceptions of American capitalism bending the rules. In the United States, too, trials of so-called "imperial CEOs," some of whom like Bernie Ebbers denied knowing anything about the companies that they were supposed to have headed, marked a turn to seek a more "American" way of doing business. The growing concern within the United States to increase control and regulation—mani-fested notably in the 2002 Sarbanes-Oxley Act—is a part of the same reaction. But as with other initiatives, the United States seeks to univer-salize the new approach, so that companies from other countries are obliged to accept the new U.S. regulatory approach if they wish to con-tinue to do business in the United States.

Big wars are very obviously catastrophes that divide and impoverish the world. The analytical puzzle of this chapter was why small-scale or limited wars (such as the Boer War or the 2003 Iraq conflict) can also have a devastating effect. The answer lies to a large extent in the way in which conflict in an era of globalization is identified with changes in business structure and business opportunities. When security issues become paramount, corporations appear to be lined up with national interests. At the same time, concentrations of economic power provoke criticism, and a backlash against powerful corporations goes alongside an attack on imperialism.

Terminus: Beyond the Fringe

THE CLASSICAL TALE of decline and fall of empires involves both strains in the center and constant erosion at the periphery. One of the great turning points in Edward Gibbon's saga occurs shortly after the death of the Emperor Julian the Apostate, one of the figures in Roman history whom Gibbon admired most. Julian's weak and short-lived successor, Jovian, concluded a peace under the terms of which the city of Nisibis as well as five Roman provinces were surrendered to the Persians. Jovian might have denounced the shameful treaty, but instead he faithfully followed its terms. According to Gibbon,

> The same motives which forced him to subscribe, now pressed him to execute the treaty of peace. He was impatient to secure the empire at the expense of a few provinces, and the respectable names of religion and honour concealed the personal fears and ambition of Jovian. . . . The predecessors of Jovian had sometimes relinquished the dominion of distant and unprofitable provinces; but, since the foundation of the city, the genius of Rome, the god Terminus, who guarded the boundaries of the republic, had never retired before the sword of a victorious enemy.[116]

After Julian, the Roman retreat began.

While it was obvious to Gibbon (thinking about North America or India) that empires are most vulnerable on their fringes, for the very modern world (with instant communications) the frontiers are everywhere. This is why, however attractive the classical analogy may be as a comparative device, the old sense of empires is completely passé. At the same time, some of the old debates about empire, in particular how prosperity and markets can be secured against "barbarians," remain quite actual. This chapter looks at the dynamics of the frontier that propelled past empires to expand, and then turns to the modern debate.

Empires are immensely sensitive to what happens at the periphery. They are defined by the frontier, and are worried by their limits. Rome was acutely aware that there was no "imperium sine fine."[117] Overextension becomes the classical trap for empires: they need to defend their prestige, the genius of Terminus, even in the distant outposts; and setbacks there look as if they challenge the whole basis of imperial rule. In a notional cost-benefit of empire, there is little direct benefit from the frontier defense, which is remote, thinly settled, and poor (if it were not, it would become central, and would then have its own surrounding carapace or periphery). On the other hand, the benefit accrues because of the implications for the defense of the whole. Imperial rulers have at the center of their imagination some domino scheme, in which a single small collapse could trigger a cycle of decay and disintegration. Does this perception reflect reality, or is it a self-induced delusion or what Jack Snyder terms a "myth of empire"?[118] Why should the participants worry at the partial or even the complete collapse of empires?

They do so because empires become encumbered by a tremendous baggage of emotion and rhetoric that reflects the circumstances in which they arise. There is never simply a crude economic driver to imperialism. The balance sheets of empires are subject to enormous distortion by their friends and their enemies, and there is a rather crude either-or analysis that is usually presented as a simple political argument. Friends of empire see their project as a civilizing mission, which produces benefits to all, including both the colonizer and the colonized. Empires are ways of introducing peace, the rule of law, prosperity. The British journalist W. T. Stead applauded Cecil Rhodes as the man destined by Providence to explain the British mission in "the upward trend of human progress." Lord Curzon held that "the British Empire is under Providence the greatest instrument for good that the world has seen," while General Smuts saw it as "the widest system of organized human freedom which has ever existed in human history." The French writer Paul Leroy-Beaulieu explained that the aim of colonization was "to make a new society in the best conditions of prosperity and progress" and that the process of colonization was "simply a temporary education of inferior peoples by superior peoples."[119]

By contrast, the liberal tradition, which is embodied in the classical American view of European imperialism and clearly owes its origins to the circumstances of 1776, is skeptical of the benefits of empire, for either the colonizer or the colonized. For the liberals, the subjects of imperialism are not the only victims of the grasping rapaciousness of empire. Liberal critics of empire see the imperial process as a lust for power and profit, which produces a systematic and dysfunctional distortion of incentives. The imperialists have a short-term horizon, in which they look for exploitative gains that harm the subjects of imperialism; and at the same time they accumulate gains that represent monopoly rents and are precarious were the monopoly to be challenged. This is the economic equivalent of the famous master and slave dialectic presented by Hegel, in which slavery dehumanizes the master as well as the object of his compulsion. For the liberal, vested interests build a strength that depends on the maintenance of imperial rule, but is inherently vulnerable.

Neither the imperialist apology nor the liberal criticism in their extreme formulation provide a way of grasping the classical geography of imperial rule: there is a core of empire, with a powerful and rational economic logic, from which the imperial hegemon derives benefits, and then around it there are gradations of usefulness. The frontier is useless from the economic viewpoint, but vital from the political and psychological perspective.

Empires usually arise in circumstances other than a systematic urge for betterment of the whole world. They stem in the most part from an accidental defense of existing positions that requires further expansion to generate sufficient security. As traders reach beyond the frontiers, their activities destabilize neighboring areas, and the resulting collapses of traditional forms of authority and the appearance of lawlessness draws out a new imperial intervention.[120] The result is that the overall cost-benefit sheet of empires looks bad, both for the imperialists and the colonized (though not necessarily, of course, for the particular groups whose power, wealth, and prestige are caught up with the forward thrust of empire).

The great European empires on the whole drew little gain from their territorial empires in the way of economic benefits during the early days of imperialism (when the first, or eighteenth-century, British Empire rose and then partially collapsed); and empires in consequence became the subject of much liberal criticism. Adam Smith, and later John

Bright and Richard Cobden, in short every respectable British liberal, piled on the critique of empire. After the Burmese war of 1852, Cobden thundered, "But it is not consistent with the supremacy of that moral law, which mysteriously sways the fate of empire, as well as of individuals, that deeds of violence, fraud and injustice, should be committed with permanent profit and advantage."[121]

The liberal strictures seem justified by the overall economic and financial calculus. In the second half of the eighteenth century, Britain probably exported products worth around 10 percent of GNP, but less than half of this went to the non-European "periphery." Profits from colonial and semicolonial trade would have been sufficient to finance only about 15 percent of the overall investment undertaken during the industrial revolution.[122]

In the British discussion of empire, however, something changed in the 1870s: in part, this was a reflection of the new industrialization of continental Europe, and of the United States, with the consequence that British business started to need to look for new markets. Empire started to have a distinctive economic appeal. British trade began to be diverted away from a global economy, and toward an imperial subsystem that it was able to control. Between 1870 and 1899, British exports to Europe and the United States fell in value by 19 percent, while exports to the white settler dominions rose by 17 percent and to tropical southern Africa and Asia by 38 percent. In the 1860s, 36 percent of British trade had been with the empire; the proportion rose to 47 percent in the 1880s and by the end of the 1920s to 59 percent.[123] Empire was thus a consolation prize for a failure to do well in a more global setting: a wooden spoon award rather than a glittering prize.

In part, the imperial idea also reflected for Britain a parallel sense of loss of influence in the international system, as Germany unified and became a Great Power posing a formidable military threat, and as Russian industrialization promised to take the tsarist empire down the same path. Queen Victoria was moved by the Asian interpretation of European events as related in a memorandum of the Persian minister: according to this, the French emperor had fought the Russian emperor in the Crimean War in order to become the "King of Kings," and then the German emperor had overthrown the French emperor in order to take the title.[124] Britain needed an imperial title as a demonstration of its power, and in 1876 the Royal Titles Act made Victoria "Empress of India."

Benjamin Disraeli's great defense of Britain as an imperial nation in the Crystal Palace speech of 1872 began with a reckoning with the cost-benefit approach to empire, and then tried to deflect British attention toward morals and politics rather than economics:

> It has been proved to us that we have lost money by our colonies. It has been shown with precise, with mathematical demonstration, that there was never a jewel in the Crown of England that was so truly costly as the possession of India. . . . [Liberals] looked even upon our connection with India, as a burden upon this country, viewing everything in a financial aspect, and totally passing by those moral and political considerations which make nations great, and by the influence of which alone men are distinguished from animals. . . . in my opinion no minister in this country will do his duty who neglects any opportunity of reconstructing as much as possible of our colonial Empire, and of responding to those distant sympathies which may become the source of incalculable strength and happiness to this land.[125]

In the long run, perhaps, empires might make for greater wealth, but the preeminent source of satisfaction would be a nonmaterial gratification of the urge to empire.

Those who wanted to benefit from empire had to demonstrate ways in which an imperial intervention to help them could be justified by overall security requirements. India could be adequately secured only by a dramatic push against rival imperial system Russia in the destabilized tribal areas of the Northwest Frontier. The defense of supply routes to India also required control of Egypt, of the strategic position on the Cape of Good Hope, and of eastern Africa.[126]

The greatest British imperialist advocate at the moment of Britain's greatest imperial reach was Joseph Chamberlain, who popularized the term *pax britannica*, with its obviously classical appeal. He was very explicit in his admission that empire was a response to economic failure (or, as he thought, to the unfair competition posed by the protected industries of Germany and the United States). In a speech at Greenock, on October 7, 1903, he mourned the obvious fact of British decline, "Agriculture . . . has practically been destroyed. Sugar has gone; silk has gone; iron is threatened; wool is threatened; cotton will go!" A year or so later, he said, "In the past this country was . . . the workshop of the world. . . . That is no longer the case. . . . Our competitors are gaining upon us in that which makes national greatness. . . . Those are the wise nations that look a little ahead and see a difficulty before it overwhelms them." The solution for Chamberlain was not a deliberate quest for material gain: rather, like Disraeli, he emphasized the intangible sides of imperialism. In Birmingham, in the heartland of English manufacturing, on November 4, 1903, he said, "I care very little whether the result will be to make this country, already rich a little richer. . . . What I care for is that this people shall rise to the height of its great mission . . . and in co-operation with our kinsmen across the seas . . . combine to make an Empire . . . greater, more united, more fruitful for good, than any Empire in human history."[127]

For France, a similar reorientation, described in parallel language, took place in the 1870s and 1880s. In 1874 Paul Leroy-Beaulieu explained in his *De la colonisation chez les peuples modernes* that colonialism extended markets and industrial civilization, and was a condition of "grandeur." Colonies and civilization could not be created by markets alone, however, and they required the action of the state. The French empire (apart from Algeria) was acquired in a way that closely mirrored the new British psychology of empire, in the late 1870s and early 1880s, as an explicit mechanism for compensating for the German defeat of 1870–71 and finding new power in a broader global context. The veteran French republican hero, Léon Gambetta, explained after France acquired Tunisia by the Treaty of Bardo that France was retaking its rank as a great power. After this success, the administration of Jules Ferry acquired territory in Indochina as a compensation for the loss of Alsace and Lorraine. As in Britain, overseas empire could make up for a relative weakening of the metropol.

It was only in the fading days of European empire, in the interwar years of the first half of the twentieth century, that empires were really called on to redress the economic deficiencies of the Old World. Britain and France tried to make up for their war-induced problems by expanding trade with and investment in their colonies. Colonies would supply raw materials, markets, as well as military manpower to mother countries that had been overstrained.

It was at this stage that colonial planning developed to its fullest extent, with bad effects on both the metropol and the subjects of imperialism. It is certainly possible to make an argument that in some initial phase of empire the extension of European rule brought some benefits: a more stable legal order, the provision of transportation networks (canals, railroads, telegraphs, road improvements), supplies of capital, and improved education. Yet the good effects were gradually overshadowed by administrative fiat and distortions, aimed at keeping a particular vision of society that corresponded to the preferences of the metropol. The effect was most striking in India, the core of Britain's nonsettler empire. Eric Hobsbawm has noted the unique position of India:

> It was, for one thing, the only part of the British empire to which laissez-faire never applied. Its most enthusiastic champions in Britain became bureaucratic planners when they went there, and the most committed exponents of political colonization rarely, and then never seriously, suggested the liquidation of British rule.[128]

In the interwar economics of imperial preference, the colonial powers and their possessions pushed prices up above those prevailing on world markets in what they saw as a cartel of mutual advantage. Economic means would be used to lock up the security gains from empire. The imperial authorities then tried to regulate the microeconomic consequences of the consequently distorted trade regimes with networks of marketing boards that controlled prices and production levels. Price controls and rationing may have represented a valid attempt to deal with the specific circumstances of wartime mobilization during the World War II; but these lessons were widely misinterpreted as a demonstration of the superiority of plans and controls. In particular, the postcolonial policymakers then drew the inappropriate conclusion that prices should be controlled to make a new political bargain: to impoverish the economically backward rural producers of commodities and to benefit a new urban class that would be the political driving force of the newly independent states. In doing this, the new rulers were simply preserving the legacy of a particular and effective technique of colonial rule: it was essential to make a compromise with powerful groups that were politically concentrated. More peripheral (and usually poorer and weaker) elements could be held in check by the occasional display of force. The worst horrors of late colonial rule and early independence were thus inflicted on the rural and the poor, as in the brutally suppressed Mau Mau revolt of Kenya, in which virtually the entire tribe was kept in concentration camps.[129]

After Indian independence, the raj gave way to the regulation raj, in which all the panoply of colonial controls were used to promote the construction of a Soviet-style heavy industrial sector supposedly to modernize India and drive out rural backwardness. In west Africa, marketing boards wrecked the hopes of African farmers.

Given this experience, it is hardly surprising that the concept of imperialism was deeply discredited by the second half of the twentieth century. Yet the problems and tensions, the volatile frontier regions, and the urge to stabilize and extend existing control and markets, that had given rise to the imperial solution in the first place still existed. They now called forth some grudging and retrospective accolades to the achievements of empire. Richard Haas in 2000, shortly before he became director of policy planning in the State Department, spoke of the need for Americans to "re-conceive their global role from one of a traditional nation-state to an imperial power" (adding, however, that "an imperial foreign policy is not to be confused with imperialism").[130]

The need could be conceived in the following way: most of the world was covered by a global economic space with flows of goods, capital, and labor stimulating a more productive use of resources, but this space was surrounded by areas barely touched by the process of "globalization" and in which ideas actively hostile to it could develop. The nonglobalized world was capable of not merely surrounding but also penetrating into the globalized core and of disrupting and potentially destroying it. The definitive demonstration of this possibility came on September 11, 2001, when what had originally been a dispute over American troops in Saudi Arabia, that had escalated out to remote mountainous areas in Afghanistan, now spilled back into the center of the globalized world—New York and Washington, D.C.

The modern threats involved the intertwining of three elements. None of them is new, but since 2001 it has become clear that they can interact in a particularly threatening and deadly way: the existence of terrorists, who want to use terror as a way of shaking the global political and economic order; the existence of weapons of mass destruction (WMD); and the presence of a substantial number of "failed states" that provide a breeding ground for lawlessness.

The leverage of terrorists has grown greater as a result of the rapidity with which information can be transmitted. The shock effect of terrorism was already evident in the last age of globalization: at the end of the nineteenth century, anarchists engaged in spectacular acts of individual terror, assassinations, such as that of French President Sadi Carnot (1894), Austrian Empress Elisabeth ("Sissi") (1898), King Umberto of Italy (1900), U.S. President McKinley (1901), or symbolic outrages such as the attempt in 1894 to blow up the Greenwich Royal Observatory at the center of the integrated time system of the world (on the first, or original, line of longitude). The shock effect depended on the way in which these events became immediate sensations, and there is not much of a gulf between the theories of terror of late-nineteenth-century anarchists and those of anti-American or Islamic terrorists today.

The existence of the Internet and other technology enabling users to send news around the world in an instant, makes it possible to influence opinions very quickly. Such opinion shifts can dramatically influence policy. One event in particular set a model for suicide bombing, the attack on October 23, 1983, which killed 241 U.S. marines serving as part of a peace-keeping multinational force in Lebanon. Despite an immediate response by President Reagan that the United States had vital interests in Lebanon and would not withdraw, within six months the remaining marines were "redeployed" and the United States effectively humiliated. The attack had showed in a striking way the vulnerability of the United States once it defined periphery as vital interest. Vulnerability, rather than interest, is the way empires usually rationalize their expansion.

The openness of empire to attack is also the wedge that terrorists then could use against what they wished to portray as a new and sinister empire. The new media offer plentiful resources for new types of propaganda. Al-Jazeera broadcasts showing horrific scenes in which hostages who have supposedly cooperated with American or British imperialists are executed can achieve an instant notoriety. A classical strategy of terrorists, already used in the anarchist practice of the late nineteenth century, is to attack not the most obviously repressive representatives of a dominant power, but softer and kinder targets, to show that terrorism can strike anywhere, and that even humane and good activity is a way of supporting repression. Thus the most striking propaganda coups of Iraqi insurgents against the U.S. military and the provisional Iraqi regime involve not so much strikes against U.S. forces but against long-established aid workers, such as the Irish-Iraqi Margaret Hassan, or critical journalists, such as the Italian Giuliana Sgrena.

The second element behind today's worldwide threats involves new types of weapons, which can be manufactured with relative ease. In the nineteenth century, the improvement of guns and explosives first made states stronger, and then gave resources to anarchist rebels. In the realist tradition, the existence of WMDs was often held to have been a stabilizing force in international relations when they were in the possession of a limited number of strong states, who could use them in the construction of a balance of terror that kept international peace.[131] But in the aftermath of the end of the Cold War, they began to proliferate. They became weapons of the weak who wanted to change the international system from the outside, rather than of the strong, who were already represented in a functioning international system. Thus countries like Japan or Italy or Germany, with high levels of economic performance and technical skill, saw no obvious point in developing atomic or chemical weapons, as they would have nothing to gain from such an acquisition.

Iraq, as a pariah since the botched conclusion of the Gulf War in 1991, became a test case for the way in which the world might respond to a weak outsider instrumentalizing the threat of WMDs. In retrospect, it appears that Iraq, which possessed chemical and biological weapons, and demonstrated its willingness to use them on insurgents within the country, in fact destroyed almost, if not all of, its WMDs in the wake of the 1991 defeat. This destruction, however, was not known or knowable, and after September 11, 2001, Iraq became a test case for the international system.

The belief in the power of Iraqi destruction underpinned the arguments of both the advocates and the critics of war. For the advocates, the preventive war argument, as explained in the September 2002 U.S. National Security Document, depended on dealing with a threat that was bound to increase. For the critics, there was a pragmatic but powerful argument against war: that it would be simply too dangerous and costly, because Iraq would unleash a fearful armory of biological and chemical weapons. A process of disarmament supervised by the United Nations held out a much more promising way of dealing with what was a real and even terrifying threat.

In retrospect, it might be said in defense of the attack on Iraq that the absence of WMDs, or at least the inability to find them easily, does not matter. It is a matter of judging intentions, which are not easy to judge in advance. We know about the failure to undertake preventive action if things turn out badly; but the simple fact of preventive action may make the object of that action look better than he should. If, for instance, France and Britain had attacked Germany in the spring of 1939 in the wake of the Czech invasion, they would easily have won militarily, but for generations Germans would be repeating the formula that Hitler did not really represent a threat to Europe. It is, unfortunately, often possible to judge the full danger of a regime only after a great deal of damage has been done.

There is another type of precedent, in that in the 1930s both Hitler and Stalin deliberately exaggerated the extent of their armaments spending and their military preparation, in the hope that this would intimidate and deter potential opponents. For Saddam Hussein, the strategy was a more complex one. Immediately after the first Gulf War, texts of his speeches circulated calling for the establishment of secret arms factories. In responding to pressure from the Clinton Administration, he called for a pan-Arab revolt against American stooges and collaborators. In the lead-up to a new war, he talked about forcing the new Mongols to commit suicide at our gates. Even when the fighting was going on, he told his people to fight with whatever was available.

All of this talk was calculatedly ambiguous. Some foreigners could dismiss it as part of an inflamed rhetorical tradition. It was clearly designed, however, to influence the outside world as well as the domestic audience. There it fitted into a new sort of rhetoric of terror. Analysts of Iraq disagreed about the appropriate reaction, but they were united in the belief that there was a real WMD issue. Saddam Hussein's regime encouraged this opinion, because it offered an effective (and very cheap) instrument of diplomacy. Saddam had a very strong motive to misrepresent his motivations.

Iraq was not unique in taking this course, which emerged as an unanticipated outcome of the collapse of the Soviet Union. One of the most frequent arguments for why Western states and financial institutions should offer generous aid to self-styled reformers was that this was the only practical way of stabilizing a dangerous nuclear arsenal. Russia successfully presented itself for a few years in the early 1990s as a special case. It was a polity that was "too nuclear to fail." At the same time, China, though growing very rapidly, was still by far the largest recipient of World Bank development support, and China based its claim on world attention in large part on its military power and its potential to destabilize the region.

The Russian and Chinese examples inevitably produced a large number of imitators. The acceleration of the nuclear weapons program in both India and Pakistan was driven by the belief that nuclearity was a prerequisite for being considered seriously by the international community. North Korea, a desperate state with a failing economy, first applied nuclear blackmail in 1994 with the thought that a calculus analogous to that applied in the former Soviet Union would bring some assistance from the outside. Iran, with a large requirement for new investment to make good the losses incurred after the Iranian Revolution, accelerated its own nuclear program.

The "axis of evil" was a product of an undesirable and dangerous linkage between nuclear armament and economic opening. In Iraq, the United States and the United Kingdom became the victims of a bluff that they had helped to frame and to which they had been a party at the beginning of the 1990s. The international community was supposed to be coerced into accommodating a threat of terror.

The experience points to a clear failure of policies and institutions in the changing international balance that followed the end of the Cold War. There is at present no institutional way of deterring nuclear blackmail. Security thinking takes place in one international forum, while economic assistance fits into the domain of the Bretton Woods institutions, which are charged to be apolitical. Though there might be a logic to combining these discussions, such a change would require a radical alteration of international rule.

Finally, the inability of some states in Africa, the Balkans, Central Asia, and Southeast Asia to maintain basic order means that they can become a center for the activity of terrorists and a source of global instability. They become the dangerous periphery of the interconnected world. In such cases, there is no longer a state monopoly of force, and criminality and disorder proliferate. The criminal gangs can operate as a funding operation for terrorists. Conventional markets cannot operate efficiently without the rule of law, and in their absence poverty and fear accelerate the social collapse. The fact of state failure may not be a general one: thus even advanced industrial countries, such as Britain or Spain, in the 1970s were unable to control parts of their respective territories, in Northern Ireland or the Basque country. So state failure may run a gamut from an inability to control some important area to the almost complete collapse of the infrastructure of government and authority, as in Ethiopia or Sudan. The modern phenomenon of the "failed state" is the clearest parallel to the world of nineteenth-century Africa or Asia, when destabilized frontier zones threatened constant incursions and thus justified action to expand empire.

There is no evidence that the "failed state" is becoming quantitatively more significant as globalization advances, but the scale of the threat becomes greater with more interdependence. The most authoritative accounts of the "failed state" phenomenon show that the number of cases of state failure was more or less constant for much of the past fifty years, surged in the later 1980s and early 1990s as the Soviet empire fell apart, but then fell off again.[132] The bloodiest civil wars of the 1990s simmered down by the next decade in Somalia, Angola, and Tajikistan. As countries become more prosperous, the risk of civil war and disintegration diminishes, and there is much evidence that this transition is already improving conditions in many areas.[133] Nevertheless, there are still "failed states" in the world of the early twenty-first century, and each poses some kind of threat.

According to one analysis, fifty out of the world's seventy low-income countries are "weak in a way that threatens U.S. and international security".[134] Civil wars tend to spill over to neighbors; and state failure becomes contagious in that it interacts with the other sources of destabilization. Some collapsed states may simply be centers of disease, but viruses and bacteria have a powerful potential to spread and impose real burdens over wide areas. It is often argued that U.N. peace-keeping troops were responsible for taking back drug-resistant strains of malaria from Laos and Cambodia to West Africa, where it has incurred terrible human costs. In other cases, criminals can set up a base from which they can raid the surrounding areas.

Big and powerful countries will disagree on which of the many candidates among the population of failed states at the moment is more of a menace. Russia sees Chechenya as a major threat; France sees North African fundamentalist extremism; the United States, Iraq. It is clearly also impossible for even a massively hegemonic power to intervene militarily in all the cases of state failure.

When one case is selected as the center of a big power's vital interests, the nineteenth-century type of mechanism laid out above comes into play: the periphery begins to be defined as the central strategic interest of the empire, to be defended at all costs, and other interests are neglected. Critics have often pointed out that this was the trap in which the United States was caught in Vietnam in the late 1960s, when the focus on Vietnam meant the neglect of opportunities to open up diplomacy with China.[135] There was a similar example of such a distortion of strategic priorities after 1979, when the Iranian hostage crisis was given such attention that the general strategic problems of the Cold War were pushed to one side. There is clearly a similar danger in focusing all of U.S. power and prestige on the outcome of an uncertain process of democratization and state-building in Iraq. The imperial challenge then begins to dislocate the articulation of overall interest and order.

Frontier in the world of today is a much more ambiguous concept, because in a world of rapid communication and travel, everywhere could be interpreted as having a frontier quality. The United States today has an advanced military capability. It spends more on defense than the next fifteen nations combined (some accounts claim than the next twenty-four countries). It has military bases all over the world: in 2003, there were 702 overseas bases in 130 countries. Critics such as Chalmers Johnson see the worldwide American "footprint" as the functional equivalent of British imperial rule: "America's version of the colony is the military base."[136] The bases are an important part of the political and economic framework of the host countries, and for the most part they are welcomed: in a world in which anti-Americanism is on the rise, the most pro-American sentiments are expressed by citizens of countries such as Panama, the Philippines, and Poland, which have very important U.S. military bases. They provide a platform for rapid intervention in crisis situations, along the lines of a famous book title of a modern bestseller *Eats, Shoots & Leaves*.[137] On the other hand, they are hardly suited to long-term interventions for the construction of a better political order.

The vision of how the world might generally be stabilized through the utilization of military power was most dramatically set out in the September 2002 National Security Strategy of the United States of America. According to this argument, the world basically wants to be peaceful, but there may be some spoilers who are prepared to inflict high costs on the rest of the world. If the rest of the world needs to spend large amounts in self-defense, it is diverting resources that could be better used to achieve basic human needs: disease eradication, the provision of infrastructure, or the alleviation of mass poverty. There is hence a case for delegating the task of dealing with threats. "The United States must and will maintain the capability to defeat any attempt by an enemy—whether a state or non-state actor—to impose its will on the United States, our allies, or our friends. We will maintain the forces sufficient to support our obligations, and to defend freedom. Our forces will be strong enough to dissuade potential adversaries from pursuing a military build-up in hopes of surpassing, or equaling, the power of the United States."[138]

Preventive interventions, however, may not necessarily provide a satisfactory basis for the creation of politically stable and successful units. At the best, they can really be only large-scale policing operations. The argument about the positive contribution of imperial rule emphasizes that empires brought basic order, literacy, and the rule of law. These may be outweighed, however, by perverse effects: that the imperial forces who enforce the laws have to take sides, and they get drawn into local and factionalized disputes. The longer empire continues, the more the perverse effects outweigh those that are beneficial.

Imperialism, even or perhaps especially in the most enlightened cases, is accompanied by extraordinary levels of violence. It is usually remembered as a series of spectacular brutalizations: the Athenian destruction of Melos, the Roman eradication of Carthage, Oliver Cromwell at

Drogheda on September 11, 1649, the German genocide of the Herreros in Southwest Africa, or the Amritsar massacre of 1919. But violence has little effect except when at least some people know about it: this was the point of the display of impaled heads in the Belgian Congo as depicted in Joseph Conrad's horrifying portrayal of the inner psychology of the *Heart of Darkness*. It is exemplary. This is the doctrine that is currently known as "shock and awe." Oliver Cromwell's epitaph on Drogheda was that it should be a lesson for posterity:

> I am persuaded that this is a righteous judgment of God upon these bar-
> barous wretches, who have imbued their hands in so much innocent blood
> and that it will tend to prevent the effusion of blood for the future, which
> are satisfactory grounds for such actions, which otherwise cannot but work
> remorse and regret.

When, however, the images of violence are distributed very widely, as they are in a modern media age, they undermine rather than strengthen the imperial power. Thus the Vietnam conflict became largely judged in terms of two widely disseminated and striking photographs, of a naked little girl running in terror down a street in a napalm attack, and of the Saigon police chief in the act of shooting a Vietcong suspect in the temple. The U.S. role in Iraq became simplified as the sadistic smiling pose of Private Lynndie England pointing at the genitals of the naked Iraqi prisoner in Abu Ghraib. The violence and humiliation that come with interventions thus became very obviously counterproductive.

With higher degrees of education and literacy, and with more widespread access to communications, the perverse effects of imperial impositions are likely to become greater, and the positive effects lesser.

The best alternatives to the question of creating political order and avoiding state disintegration and failure are the establishment of regional poles of stability and the generation of institutional mechanisms on a worldwide level. At the heart of these solutions is the linkage between, on the one hand, economic reform and increased prosperity, and, on the other, political reforms that create legitimacy through representative institutions.

Thus the United States has been a pole of stability for Mexican politics, offering access to markets (for goods and labor), as well as a model for political pluralism. Stability in post-apartheid South Africa sets a model for other countries in southern Africa. The European Union has played a similar role with respect to the stabilization of politics in Central and Eastern Europe in the wake of the collapse of communism. The availability of a model, and the prospect of deriving benefits by integration, discredited radical and nationalistic policies. Former communists embraced the market and democracy, while nationalists such as Slovakia's would-be strongman Vladimir Meciar were pushed out. There is clear evidence of a simple geographic causality: the nearer physically to the European Union, the greater the stabilization effect of political life.[139] The European Union may also be able to take a similar role in regard to North Africa. Where big regional powers do not take on a stabilizing function—as is the case for such powerful and potentially rich oil producers as Nigeria in West Africa or Saudi Arabia in the Middle East—failed states quickly develop around the periphery.

The stumbling block on the way to stabilizing order are memories of the past. Thus in North Africa, unlike in Central Europe, there is a paralysis induced by the legacy of empire. France may bring good will to modern Algeria or Morocco, but that good will is continually undercut by memories of empire. It is as if the world expected post-Soviet Russia to play the leading role in reshaping central Europe in a liberal, democratic, and market-oriented reform process. Such an experiment could not really be expected to carry any conviction, and would likely be counterproductive.

A second mechanism involves taking some of the strain off the political process in potentially unstable societies by importing legitimacy from the outside, through a worldwide system of incentives. The dilemma is that markets need strong institutional frameworks, but at the same time rapid changes of income and wealth that accompany market expansion can undermine the legitimacy of weak institutions. International institutions are a powerful and effective way of establishing credibility, above all because they bring a greater element of a rule-based approach. Countries that want to stabilize themselves, reduce poverty, open their economies, and achieve higher growth find plenty of obstacles in their way, especially if they are embarking at the same time on experiments with political reform and democratization. Though there is an ample literature on the overall beneficial effects of trade liberalization, there are many vested interests in the existing protected industries that are threatened.

Avoiding state and societal failure, or recovering from it, is an inherently precarious process. Outside observers have sometimes as a result concluded that autocracies, such as Chile under General Pinochet, or Singapore under Lee Kuan Yew, or even the People's Republic of China under a decaying party rule, could do better than a more liberal or democratic regime.

But this is a misreading of the options available. Substantial political tensions build up even in relatively benign autocracies such as Mahathir Mohamad's Malaysia. The interventions of the Communist Party in corporate governance have been a source of weakness and not strength for China. Where rule is more unpredictable, the results are much worse. Harsh autocracies such as that of General Mobutu in Zaire impose a multitude of distortions and set off some of the mechanisms that eventually lead to state failure.

The regimes of precariously balanced states thus need some sort of external mechanism for promoting stability. One very obvious and easy mechanism is to justify an economic reform program by claiming that it is imposed from the outside, and hence not subject to political choice or debate. The outside agency is then used as a defusing mechanism or lightning rod to conduct harm away from the political process. In interwar Europe, the League of Nations was used in this manner, to impose highly unpopular and deflationary stabilization programs on Austria and Hungary. In 1948 Germany, the Western Allies took something of this role when they determined to impose a radical, and initially highly unpopular, currency reform. From the 1960s, the role of scapegoat in the reform exercise often fell to the Bretton Woods institutions, the World Bank and the International Monetary Fund. But such a device cannot be overused without discrediting it. Antagonism toward the IMF in cases such as 1970s Jamaica or post-2000 Argentina certainly provided an instrument for political alliance formation and even political stabilization, but it did so on the basis of a dysfunctional populist nationalism.

A milder version of the same process of stabilization from the outside involves the provision of expert advice as a way of bridging political divisions, or overcoming bureaucratic hurdles. The outsider can be a management consultant, and indeed some analogy from the business world may help to show how the mechanism may be most effective.

Since what the consultants say may well be a familiar song to many of the domestic participants in the reform process, and the real problems are internal political obstacles, the credibility of the outside agent is crucial. Thus being paid (well) is an important part of the consultation process for the management adviser (in a similar way as it may be for a pyscho-therapist at the level of individuals). For countries dealing with international financial institutions, the cost of the advice is not so much a fee as the acceptance of conditionality.

The essence of the stabilization gambit is that it should find a way of establishing restraints on the political process so that an explosion of demands does not undermine stability. Fareed Zakaria recently concluded that it has become more important to restore the rule of law than it is to build democracy.[140] He is consciously reviving an old debate that goes back to Alexis de Tocqueville on the mutual incompatibility of democracy and liberalism. Many nineteenth-century liberals were terrified by the prospect of a mob rule that would destroy property and order, and make abstract law impossible.

In practice, however the rule of law is impossible without a measure of consensus, and that consensus can best be achieved by the institutions of democratic practice. The *demos* has a responsibility, but of a general kind, for the political and economic order, while it needs to avoid micro-interventions. In many cases, this *demos* needs additional help, and this is what can be provided by a well-constructed international system, and only by an international system interacting with and extending domestic political community.

The core of such an international system is a rule-based process that makes it less vulnerable to the charge of being a new form of imperialism or neocolonialism. Rules may be a way of ensuring that "the genius of Terminus" does not in practice terminate experiments in the extension of the principles of legal certainty and order.

The Holy Roman Empire and
the Roman Empire

THE READINESS with which critique of empires is formulated suggests that there can and should be an alternative. The most obvious contemporary candidate for a global model of nonimperial political and constitutional experiment is Europe. Indeed there is an undercurrent of publications, emanating almost entirely from American critics of American power, from Charles Kupchan's *The End of the American Era: U.S. Foreign Policy and the Geopolitics of the Twenty-first Century* (2002) through Jeremy Rifkin's *The European Dream* (2004) to T. R. Reid's *The United States of Europe: The New Superpower and the End of American Supremacy* (2004), and Mark Leonard's *Why Europe Will Run the Twenty-First Century* (2005), which claim that Europe is developing into an effective counterweight to the imperial hegemonic claims of the United States.[141] Europe does this not because it is economically more efficient, or harder working, or because it wields military power more effectively (any of these arguments would be risible) but because the European project is based on a fundamentally superior set of values.

There is, however, a problem in defining these values, and in demonstrating or proving their superiority. Europeans often put the case in a different way, claiming that they have evolved a better political process. Europe in particular thinks that it has a more consensual way of making rules. This in reality reflects not so much the superiority of a legislative process, but rather the absence of one. Most European legislation comes as a consequence of a European Court of Justice ruling that legislative decisions of the Council of Ministers had automatic effect in member countries. Legislation thus emerges out of a complicated and slow-moving set of intergovernmental negotiations, with the result that it does not seem threateningly imperial.

Europeans also occasionally think that they have through this process evolved a model with widespread applicability outside Europe. The new or potential economic superpowers, particularly, India or China, are multilingual, have a complicated government structure, and in addition require a security concept that can be enlarged to encompass volatile neighbors. Europe seems to hold a template for solutions to such problems.

Historically, there is certainly an alternative to the debate about revival of the Roman imperium. It developed in great part on the geographic base of the old empire: that of the Holy Roman Empire. The idea of a special European option is not just a product of the intense discussion that followed after September 11, 2001, and especially after the Iraq war. On the contrary, it has very old historical roots. The British Prime Minister Harold Macmillan, in the course of an altercation with General de Gaulle, once stated, "You want to rebuild the Holy Roman Empire. We, the Roman Empire!"[142]

What did Macmillan mean? While the values associated with Rome evoke the idea of sovereignty, in the world of the Holy Roman Empire sovereignty is fragmented and diffused. The sovereign cannot be located. Samuel Pufendorf, who in the seventeenth century tried to expound a neatly Hobbesian theory of sovereignty for continental European consumption, in consequence found the Holy Roman Empire to be an irregular and unnatural object (*irregulare aliquod corpus*), or like a "monster" (*monstro simile*), ungraspable in theoretical terms and by the eighteenth century a popular verdict as formulated by Voltaire was that this political form was not holy, not Roman, and obviously not an empire. Gibbon was pretty skeptical too. At the end of *Decline and Fall,* as he takes his leave from the Western Roman empire, he quotes the humanist Aeneas Sylvius describing what Gibbon calls "the repellent state of Christendom":

It is a body without a head; a republic without laws or magistrates. The pope or the emperor may shine as lofty titles, as splendid images; but they are unable to command, and none are willing to obey: every state has a separate prince, and every prince a separate interest. What eloquence could unite so many discordant and hostile powers under the same standard? Could they be assembled in arms, who would dare to assume the office of general? What order could be maintained? . . . Who would understand their various languages, or direct their stranger and incompatible manners?[143]

Gibbon then points out that this critic, Aeneas Sylvius, as Pope tried to lead Europe on a crusade against the Turks.

By a peculiar sort of historical reincarnation, the modern self-image of the European Union reproduces the discussions that took place around the curiously divided sovereignty of the Holy Roman Empire. The result of its odd constitution was that the old Holy Roman Empire did not think about military expansion, and it fostered social networks that reached out across territorial divisions. Its attractions depended on what would now be termed (in the phrase of Joseph Nye) "soft power," offering institutionalized forms of collaboration and identity. It appears breathtakingly modern, or perhaps even postmodern.

Modern Europe is similarly diverse, and because of its diversity it places a high value on solidarity and consensus. In consequence, it is slow moving and reluctant to undertake radical structural reform as promptly and as thoroughly as its critics would want. The phrase that the economist Montek Singh Ahluwahlia devised to characterize the modern Indian peculiarity might be applied as well to Europe: there is a strong consensus for weak policy reform.[144]

To some people, the sluggishness of consensus formation is inappropriate in a world in which technological change, fast communications, and globalization seem to demand fast responses and rapid policy initiatives. To its defenders, however, these slower characteristics make Europeanism profoundly reassuring: it is a sort of comfort blanket that envelops a population otherwise exposed to the wild ups and downs of the globalization ride. The differences about whether the European preoccupation with slow change is desirable clearly reflect alternative ways of managing the cost of change. Taking off from an argument derived from psychological observation that the cost of losing something is much higher than the value of acquiring the same object, Europeans conclude that it is better to restrict change for the sake of stability rather than purposely create instability to make more wealth and generate economic growth.[145]

The lack of neatness or clarity about sovereignty gives European rules a complexity that critics complain invites a rather different response than that of the U.S. system. The U.S. approach provokes anti-imperial revolt and protest, while the European complex answer to the process of how to make rules leads to bewilderment and disobedience. The German social critic Hans Magnus Enzensberger recently concluded that modern Europe was undergoing a process of "Italianization." He meant that the thicket of rules is so dense, untransparent, and even contradictory that citizens are tempted to ignore them or to simply choose those they happen to like.[146] There is actually a powerful historical and cultural precedent for such a response to complexity.

The Holy Roman Empire—which became a by-word for the impossibility of radical change—was not exactly the heir to the Roman Empire: it owed its origins to the division of Charlemagne's empire in the Treaty of Verdun (843) into a western kingdom (which would become France) and an eastern territory. It lasted until it was dissolved in 1806 in the wake of the defeat of the last emperor (Francis) by Napoleon's armies. Throughout its history it had a judicial system, albeit one that functioned often rather slowly and imperfectly (but in this it was quite characteristic of most early modern states); a system for electing an emperor by the votes of the seven, and later eight, most important territorial rulers; and an implicit (but sometimes violated) understanding that parts of the empire should not go to war with each other. The component parts of the empire varied in size from micro-states, which in some cases comprised only half a village, to quite powerful states such as Brandenburg-Prussia, Saxony, or Bavaria. From the Peace of Westphalia (1648), the larger states liked to think of themselves as fully sovereign, and Prussia in particular evolved an alliance system to oppose that of the Austrian territories, whose ruler in practice was by now always elected as Holy Roman Emperor. For Central Europeans, the Holy Roman Empire is what preceded the modern nation-state, which was brought about in part by and in part as a reaction against the French Revolution and Napoleon. It remained a mental map or template against which the present could be judged.

This ideal was revived at moments when the nation-state was felt to be inadequate. At the beginning of the twentieth century, many commentators started to argue that the nation-state was the product of a particular moment of social organization, when the ideas of the French Revolution established national citizenship, and when railroads created national markets. But as people moved across national frontiers, and as markets became broader, in short as the very powerful late-nineteenth-century form of globalization developed, the nation-state looked confining, and ambitious planners looked to wider areas.

The most well-known of these discussions in early-twentieth-century Austria and Germany involved the elaboration of a concept of "Mitteleuropa" or Central Europe. Its most articulate exponent was the Protestant liberal writer, Friedrich Naumann, whose book on *Mitteleuropa* was published during the World War I, in 1915. Naumann was not a conventional nationalist, and neither was he simply a bellicose proponent of Prussian militarist ideas. On the contrary, he and other propagandists for the idea of Central Europe emphasized its ideal and nonmilitary character. He included a paean of praise to the Metternichian concept of an alternative to the nation as a way of organizing political life. Metternich's Habsburg monarchy was "less military than Prussia, less patriarchal than old Bavaria. It was in its way a civilising influence, and considering its circumstances, modern in spirit."[147] Prenational Austria could offer a model for a postmodern state, in which a supranational bureaucracy could plan and modernize. Naumann continued to draw inspiration from the Habsburg model: "a polyglot parliamentary system, incapable of stable majorities, strengthens the bureaucracy, which with some skill and a few recurrent favours always plays off the disputants one against the other."[148] Naumann's projected state would be able to reorganize social life, drawing in the latest—at that time American—models of organization: "We must speed up those who are lingering in the old habits of work, so that they approximate to the labour rhythm of the progressive."[149] This was explicitly designed to appear as both a possibility for enrichment and a romantic quest. It could not simply be a matter of cold-blooded materialist calculation. "To enter the economic system of Mid-Europe is a soul-transforming decision." It would be a synthesis of the rational Prussian and Protestant work-obsessed North and the more casual and inspirational artistic romanticism of Catholic Vienna: "If we can unite our respective abilities, then and for the first time the hard North German civilisation will secure by your assistance that touch of charm which will make it tolerable to the outside world."[150] The

German-Austro-Hungarian union would establish the basis for a new sort of political form that could subsequently be expanded.

A similar ideal was resurrected in quite different political circumstances after the World War II, when again the nation-state appeared largely discredited and obsolete. The German Resistance circle around Helmuth James Graf von Moltke, the so-called Kreisauer Kreis, came to this conclusion: "The free and peaceful development of national culture is incompatible with the retention of absolute sovereignty by each individual state. Peace demands the creation of an order that spans the separate states." Jean Monnet, the principal architect of a supranational postwar European order, reported the justification of his project in an overheard cafe conversation: "With the Schuman plan, one thing is certain: we shall not have to go to war."[151]

The most obvious analogy between the historical Holy Roman Empire and the post-1945 construction of a European political body lies in the constitutional openness, or what Joseph Weiler has termed "mutual constitutional toleration." Nation-states are often assumed to have a similar form, but the European Union can put up with a very wide variety of constitutional practices. Some of its members, such as Spain or the United Kingdom, cannot really be considered as classical nation-states, while power in the French Republic–the classic case of the postrevolutionary nation-state—is highly centralized. The European Union has been at its most successful when it offered a room for the devolution of authority to regions. It was the adoption of a statute of autonomy (in 1979) giving a large measure of self-rule to Catalonia, as well as membership in the European Community (from 1986) that allowed Spain to achieve a great measure of stability in the aftermath of the collapse of General Franco's dictatorship. The European Union is the framework that allowed a partial unwinding of the British Union, with a move to Welsh autonomy and Scottish devolution.

Since the 1970s, the European Union (at that time called the European Community) has been expanding. The attraction that it offers to new members has been an important element in creating greater political stability. This was true for the three post-dictatorial Mediterranean countries that joined in the 1980s, Greece and then Portugal and Spain. It was also the case for the ex-communist Central European states that joined in 2004: the Czech Republic, Estonia, Hungary, Latvia, Lithuania, Poland, Slovakia, and Slovenia; and it might be true in the future for Turkey or Ukraine or even Russia. The demand for such an externally acquired stabilization becomes greater the more precarious the situation. The chief reason given why Turkey should become a member of the European Union is that it is a Muslim country in which a precarious secularism has been established, and that a consolidation of this achievement would be a model for the rest of the Islamic world. When the presidential election in Ukraine in 2004 was obviously manipulated, and the Russian Federation intervened to support its candidate, the European Union's foreign policy spokesman Xavier Solana played a crucial role in lending external support to the democratic protesters in Kiev. Europe has a clear comparative advantage in some aspects of soft power, and Andrew Moravcsik has recently claimed that "arguably the single most powerful policy instrument for promoting peace and security in the world today . . . is the ultimate in market access: admission to or association with the EU trading bloc."[152]

Yet this dynamic of Europe-endowed stability certainly also applied as much, if not even more so, to the earliest members, who made the first steps to integrate in the European Coal and Steel Community just seven years after the end of war, with its dictatorship and occupation, that had produced bitter political polarization.

The early makers of Europe conceived of their project in redemptive and quasi-theological terms: Germany, the source of the Nazi evil, could only be redeemed by an association with the countries that had been the victims of its policies. Charles de Gaulle later saw France as having a unique role, because France had suffered most: only in France had a legitimate government remained and collaborated with the German occupiers. Consequently only liberated France could "lift Germany up from her decadence." In the 1980s, the admission of new Mediterranean democracies—Greece and then Spain and Portugal, that only a few years earlier had freed themselves from military authoritarian rule—again showed how Europe could be used to overcome the legacy of the past. It is possible to see something of an analogous political theology of redemption to that outlined by de Gaulle in the admission of the formerly communist countries who had suffered while Western Europe had advanced. Indeed an analogous argument can be made for the admission of countries with Islamic traditions as a way of healing the Muslim-Christian rift. The positive view of the European project sees it as a mechanism for the transcendence of those divides that had destroyed European civilization: in the twentieth century, but perhaps also in the modern era. In this way it represents a sort of reversal of history, in which ideals and structures are used as a pincer to trap the ghosts of the past.

The pincer is actually quite a real and practical one. The real operation of European redemption lies in the binding of politics through commitments to observe democratic practices and the rule of law. These restraints remove some possibilities and hence some pressures from day-to-day politics. Such a use of supranational or international institutions is a quite common one for overburdened political systems, and the most common (and stricter) application is when developing countries use organizations such as the International Monetary Fund as a way of explaining to an electorate the ineluctability of unpleasant choice.

The most creative and thoughtful of the architects of modern Europe saw and continue to see their work as the establishment of a political form that goes beyond the traditional nation-state and the notions of sovereignty that dominated political discussion in the nineteenth and twentieth centuries. The British diplomat Robert Cooper tries to distinguish three types of political formation in the globalized chaos of the early twenty-first century. There are failed and chaotic states. There is the modern sovereign state, that on a large scale can be called an empire. And then there are postmodern entities. The latter are more innovative because they can harness a wider range of social energy. Cooper argues that "empires are ill-designed for promoting change." After 1989, with the Cold War fizzling out, Europe could at long last emancipate itself from "the imperial urge" that it itself had first produced and then had imposed on it from Moscow and Washington. The postmodern state, best realized in the European context, replaces traditional concerns with security policy and raison d'état. As Cooper explains,

The individual has won and foreign policy is the continuation of domestic concerns beyond national boundaries and not vice versa. Individual consumption replaces collective glory as the dominant theme of national life. War is to be avoided: acquisition of territory by force is of no interest.[153]

It is probably unwise to speculate too much as to whether the European preferences for diffused sovereignty and slower decision-making are really a teleological advance. They certainly reflect a different balancing point in the trade-off between efficiency and stability. It is certainly not clear that a postmodern Europe is really better at the making or implementing of desired changes (such as the implementation of the economic reform aspects of the Lisbon Agenda of March 2000). Indeed in March 2005, a European summit almost explicitly renounced the implementation of the Lisbon Agenda when it rejected a liberalizing initiative on trade in services in the European Union. The major old industrial economies, France and Germany, which had been at the center of the original impulse to integrate, were faced with great domestic political strains, and their governments worried that a short-term rise in unemployment that might follow the implementation of freer trade in services would lead to a disintegration of the governments.

The new Europe as idealized by its advocates needs to elaborate an idea that embodies its new quality. There are three alternative paths in conceiving of Europe as a new and superior form of social organization that have dominated the recent discussions: as a way of transcending market economics; as a model of the peaceful solution of conflicts; and as an alternative to less desirable forms of political existence.

First, Europe is presented as an alternative to the market. This was most obvious in the 1950s, when most observers believed that the anarchy of capitalism would produce only a repetition of the collapses and depressions of the interwar era, and would thus destroy any attempt to restore democracy or a liberal order. The economic requirement was for a plan that would coordinate the politically sensitive heavy industries of Europe, which had also been the sinews of war and conflict. The backdrop to a new momentum toward European integration from the middle of the 1980s was an increased importance of cross-national market transactions on a world scale, or what is now usually referred to as "globalization." European integration was a way of making globalization less harmful, and establishing protective mechanisms. The American utopian commentator Jeremy Rifkin sees the European reaction as an attempt to rescue the state from the destruction of welfare state regimes that had played such a prominent part in the reconstruction of Europe after the World War II. "There was a real sense of dread among policy makers in the 1980s and 1990s that government was quickly imploding and that the capitalist marketplace might eventually end up as the unchallenged arbiter of human relationships."[154] Denunciations of capitalism became a commonplace of European politics. Politicians such as Jacques Chirac, who in the 1980s had built their reputations as market advocates in the style of Margaret Thatcher, began to hurry to express their sympathies with anti-globalization protesters. In 2001, he went out of his way to say that the demonstrators in Genoa had a point: "One hundred thousand people don't get upset unless there is a problem in their hearts and spirits." By 2005, he was explaining that "ultra-liberalism is the new communism."[155]

The 2004 draft European constitution aimed at cementing Europe's new identity, and tried to maintain a very delicate balance on the issue of the market. On the one hand, it was clear that the new wave of dynamism since the 1980s has been a consequence of the embrace of the idea of a single market, as provided in the 1986 Single European Act. The move to monetary union in the 1990s established an operating trans-European capital market, which greatly facilitated the modernization and rationalization of business structures. The draft treaty listed (in Article I-4) the first "fundamental freedom": "The free movement of persons, services, goods and capital, and freedom of establishment shall be guaranteed within and by the Union." On the other hand, the treaty was full of invocations of ways of controlling and regulating and harnessing the market. The objectives, spelled out before the "fundamental freedoms" in Article I-3, included not only (paragraph 2) "an internal market where competition is free and undistorted," but also (paragraph 3) that "[t]he Union shall work for sustainable development of Europe based on balanced economic growth and price stability, a highly competitive social market economy, aiming at full employment, and social progress, and with a high level of protection and improvement of the quality of the environment. It shall promote scientific and technical advance." Nevertheless, the draft was still attacked—for instance by former

Prime Minister Laurent Fabius and a large part of the French socialist party—as being too sympathetic to the institution of the market. It was criticism from the left that led to the rejection of the constitutional treaty in the French and Dutch referenda in 2005.

Another way of making the non-market point is to claim that Europe is about the establishment of "networks." International cooperation involves, in this view, specific supranational agencies that facilitate the work of government networks "through provision of a structure within which networks of national officials can operate most effectively."[156] The idea of a network society as the most appropriate response to the information age (and as an alternative to anarchic individualistic market capitalism) was pushed in a number of reports by the European Commission, such as that of 1994, *Europe's Way to the Information Society: An Action Plan.* Programs for educational reform stressed the formation of transnational networks between universities and research institutes. Again, consciously or unconsciously there were historical models: the medieval and early modern European university was also firmly embedded in Europe-wide networks. Erasmus of Rotterdam (whose name was used for one of the big exchange scholarship programs) built up a wide range of contacts who exchanged views and traveled, and in this way they created a universal or at least European community of letters. Scholars moved quickly and freely from one university to another. By contrast, in the nineteenth century, universities were firmly built into the cause of promoting national identity and national scholarship.

The modern version of the European dream presents an ambiguous face. Any network has people who are centrally placed in the middle of all the contacts and links, but there is also a fringe where the links are less dense, and the individuals more remote and isolated. Jeremy Rifkin concludes with the optimistic version that contacts can be intensified:

> In a globalized economy where everyone is connected and ever more interdependent, the idea of autonomous free agents maximizing their individual self-interests in simple exchange transactions in markets seems woefully out of date. A network, in a very real sense, is the only corporate model capable of organizing a world of such speed, complexity, and diversity. . . . The European Union is the most advanced example of the new transnational

governing model, and for that reason, its successes and failures are being closely watched in every region of the world as nation-state leaders rethink the art of governance in a global era.[157]

The problem lies in the fact that though a network may be an organizational device, it lacks precisely the universality of rules that makes the enterprise legitimate or acceptable. Those outside the network, or even on its more distant fringes, see instead of efficient functioning, systems of friends or clientage and patronage networks. They complain about a lack of transparency and, when they transpose their argument into political terms, a lack of democratic accountability. This has been the constant theme of critics of the European Union.

Secondly, Europe offers a different answer to security issues: the European ideal is the ideal of peace, hammered out after the long and destructive European civil war or "thirty years war" of the first half of the twentieth century, 1914 to 1945. Again, this theme was laid out prominently in the new constitutional draft: the first of the Union's stated "objectives" is "to promote peace, its values and the well-being of its peoples" (Article I-3, paragraph 1).

Like the approach to the question of the market, there is a careful ambiguity about what peace means. Does it mean renouncing war as an instrument of policy, or alternatively accepting that sometimes military force is needed to keep peace? Some Europeans see that they should choose one of these positions and pursue it with ardor and tenacity, but most try to avoid making precisely such a choice.

During the Cold War, this was an easier conjuring trick to manage than after 1989–91, in that the balance of power was external to Europe, and was the product of the interplay between Washington and Moscow. In consequence, global politics gave rise to the powerful sensibility that the United States and the Soviet Union, as superpowers, were not embraceable within the European vision. In fact, in the 1980s, many major West European thinkers were very keen not even to contemplate the possibility that Central and Eastern Europe might be "European," because such thinking would involve an entanglement with conventional security thinking. During the Cold War, especially in the latter stages, West European elites and thinkers closed themselves off from what was taking place in the half of the continent dominated by the Soviet Union, behaving as if Eastern Europe were really another continent. This reflex persisted after the geopolitical watershed of 1989–91. Problems in North Korea or Iran were treated as if they were in a geopolitically distinct world. There was little interest in Turkey as a key to Central Asia. Many Americans would interpret their country's greater engagement with global problems as an awareness of the complex interrelationship of the modern world. At the same time as they performed this mental act of exclusion, the Europeans (and particularly their governments) were happy to think of the reassurance given by membership in the North Atlantic Treaty Organization. Even France, which left the military organization of NATO in 1965, continued to be a member. The security link could thus operate on a quite separate dimension to the forging of transnational economic and legal ties.

Given this background, it was probably not surprising that "Europe" as an institutionalized foreign policy system mishandled many of the issues of the 1990s, in particular those arising out of the disintegration of Yugoslavia. In imposing an arms embargo (as an exercise in the new politics of peace) on Bosnia, Europe in practice unilaterally helped Serbs in the remaining Yugoslav Federation and in Bosnia. The strongest case made by American critics of European inability to do power politics arises out of the Bosnian tragedy, and by the end of the twentieth century the complaint turned into a constant American chorus about alleged European pusillanimity. Only with U.S. intervention, in particular the campaign of air attacks on Serb positions, was it possible to start an effective negotiation on the Bosnian question, and to maintain the pressure on Milosevic and the Serbs that eventually produced the Dayton Accords. Much of the American critique, however, became quite rapidly outdated. By the time of the 1999 Kosovo crisis, though, it seemed that many European governments had absorbed the lesson of Bosnia, and they began to evolve a moral case for intervention based on the legacy of European history.

Yugoslavia is such a damning indictment that it is easy to think that the European story of the 1990s is nothing but a failure. Yet the surprising transition of almost all the other European former communist dictatorships to a new and more-or-less liberal political order, and to market economics, is a stunning success (and an obvious contrast with the isolated disaster cases of Cuba or North Korea). The avoidance of clashes in the "velvet divorce" between Czechs and Slovaks, the peacefulness of Slovenia, the stability of the Baltic states despite large ethnic Russian populations who might be expected to be unhappy with their new subordinate status in linguistically quite nationalistic states—these are all a testimony to the power of the European magnet.

Modern Europe is, in other words, a sort of empire that has a clear momentum to continuous expansion, which clearly changes quite dramatically as a consequence of the absorption of new members. It is empire by invitation, though, not by military conquest. Again, there are Habsburg overtones: it was always said that Habsburg expansion took place not through war, but as a consequence of dynastic marriage. *Tu felix Austria nube.* An important part of the modern European momentum is the recognition (so far admittedly only theoretical) that any member country can also leave the European Union. This presents a dramatic contrast with the American constitutional tradition, in which secession was not permitted and was indeed a cause of war.

Expansion of a new sort of political form based on voluntarism and the attraction of a common prosperity is sometimes held out as a generalizable model for better global governance. But attempts to imitate the European development in Africa, South America, or Asia have been largely abortive. This is because the voluntarism actually rests on rather peculiar and chance conditions, which are not easily reproducible.

In practice, for much of its history the development of the European Union depended on a dynamic in which there were four large states with a roughly similar population and economic weight (France, Germany, Italy, and the United Kingdom) who could balance each other. At the core of this relationship, there was an axis between the West German capital Bonn and Paris. The critical moment of consolidation of the European project was the Elysée Treaty of 1963 (whose anniversary was lavishly celebrated in 2003). For General de Gaulle, this relationship looked like a balance between German economic power and a traditional French emphasis on security issues. The bilateral Franco-German approach as an initiator behind European moves to integration was also behind the move to establish a European Monetary System in 1978–79. The dance of the two within the quartet looked much clumsier in the 1990s, however. The unification of West and East Germany in 1990 threw this balance off by making Germany larger, and (it appeared at the time) more economically dominant. This consideration then gave an impetus to a new push for further integration, in particular the move to monetary union, as well as to expansion. By the time the new wave of expansion in 2004 embraced twenty-five members, the Franco-German relationship looked much less central. It was marginalized by the massive addition of new political force.

Europe also suffered from a very vivid demonstration of the difficulty of enforcing apparently arbitrary rules in the absence of either a powerful hegemon or an agreement on the value basis of the rules. As part of the process of monetary union in the wake of the 1992 Maastricht Treaty, a so-called Stability and Growth Pact gave strict but apparently arbitrary maxima for public sector deficits (3 percent of GDP) and outstanding debt (60 percent of GDP). But when most of the large member states broke the rules, the President of the Commission started to refer to the pact as absurd, and a 2005 summit formally modified the rule so as to make it more-or-less capable of being stretched.

Outside Europe, it is hard to see that, for all the enthusiasm for regional integration and cooperation, such a mechanism, depending as it does on a complex and intricate out of political power balancing, can be replicated. In particular there is a substantial and growing interdependence between Japan and China, in which China is an important market for Japanese engineering and machine tools, and an outlet for Japanese investment; but it is permeated by constant political suspicion, and in particular fears about the unequal demographic weight of the countries. It is hard to imagine the 1950s European scenario taking place with a France that was ten times bigger than Germany.

Thirdly, Europe can probably most easily be defined by what its makers think it is not. It is not empire and it is not America. In doing this, modern Europeans unconsciously or consciously take up a potent type of ideology that was central in the nineteenth-century creation of nationalism. Especially the larger nations, as they were envisaged by nineteenth-century nationalistic ideologues, were quite diverse and had quite different cultural traditions. Some had different religions. In such cases—and this development was most conspicuous in Germany—the nation could most easily be defined by what it was not. German nationalists sometimes looked to an idealized version of the past, to the German forest or the gothic cathedral; but they also emphasized that they opposed French culture, French fashions, and French ideas.

The late-twentieth-century equivalent to this nineteenth-century use of culture to promote new social integration in national forms was best developed in a widely influential theory of the European left that then developed into the main stream of European thought. The Marxist writer Antonio Gramsci, imprisoned by Mussolini, was fascinated by the nineteenth-century precedent, and by the process through which a particular social group took charge of making the nation-state. He derived from this analysis the notion that culture could be used to make rules work or, as he put it, to "establish hegemony." A broad part of the left, in Italy and elsewhere, inspired by Gramsci, came to the conclusion that ideas and cultural production could be used to fight off American hegemony. Americans had economic power, and they also propagated a set of alluring cultural norms around the idea of consumption that helped them to consolidate their economic power and political influence. The European answer should be to mobilize a set of alternative norms, which might claim to be older or superior. The Gramscian answer, that the European Left should mobilize cultural capital against economic capital, appeared to be most attractive whenever the United States was acting most like an imperial power: in other words, during the Vietnam era, and then in 2003, in the lead-up to and the aftermath of the Iraq war.

The Gramscian impulse has not just been a characteristic of a cultural Left. A need to compensate for American mistakes or to resist American policies has in practice often been behind the momentum to create new European institutions. The European Monetary System in 1979 was in large part a response to the mismanagement and weakness of the U.S. dollar in the late 1970s. These were initiatives of policy-making elites frustrated by American high-handedness or incompetence; but the European response ran largely along technocratic lines.

It is only relatively recently that commentators have thought that they observed a more deeply embedded transcontinental assertion of a new identity. European civil society was mobilized by resistance to the 2003 Iraq war. One analysis, initially set out by a former French finance minister, Dominique Strauss-Kahn, spoke of the mass demonstrations against the Iraq war across Europe on Saturday, February 15, 2003, as the sign of the new civic consciousness. "A new nation was born in the street. And that new nation was the European nation."[158] Within weeks, the philosophers Jacques Derrida and Jürgen Habermas tried to coordinate a press campaign, launched simultaneously in the leading European newspapers. Habermas argued that the United States had as a consequence of its engagement in Iraq lost its "moral capital."[159] By 2005, President Chirac was appealing for a "yes" vote in the French referendum on the European constitution on the grounds that it offered a defense against America, and that the "Anglo-Saxons" were trying to frustrate a new Europe. "What is the interest of the Anglo-Saxon countries and particularly the US? It is naturally to stop Europe's construction, which risks creating a much stronger Europe tomorrow."[160]

The element of consensus was an anti-Americanism, which actually had deep historical roots (as Andrei Markovits has recently demonstrated in a brilliant historical account). America was vulgar, rich, and materialist, and even American religion was undermined by materialism. The German poet Heinrich Heine concluded, "Secular utility is the real religion, and money is their [American] god, the only all-powerful god."[161] American universalism was a duplicitous cover for the pleading of American special interests. The pursuit of profit by American corporations was given a mask of a universal crusade.

The European ideal was thus quite explicitly contrasted with the American approach. The difference has been memorably cast by Robert Kagan as Europeans coming from Venus and wanting love, while Americans come from Mars and like wars. This is an adaptation of a popular American psychological study (by John Gray) that purports to show how and why men and women can never understand each other. Or alternatively, Kagan tries to suggest that Europeans have taken the Kantian tradition seriously, while the United States is Hobbesian. To some extent Europeans attribute their preference for peace to the legacy of the wars of the first half of the twentieth century. In part, this preference also reflects the perception of West Europeans about the unique success of the second half of the century. Often, they thought of their singular stability by deliberately cutting themselves off from problems in other parts of the world. Europe's relationship to the rest of the world could be defined through its opposition to the "fundamentalisms" of radical Islam or evangelical revivalism in America and born-again Christianity in the White House.

At the same time as Europeans were trying to grasp where their "identity" lay, they formulated it more aggressively in self-consciously anti-religious terms. In doing this, they abandoned the constitutional toleration that had been a hallmark of previous European development. Joseph Weiler, probably the most astute commentator on this development, argued that if the European constitutional treaty prepared in 2004 had grown out of the previous tradition, it would have been religiously tolerant.[162] It might have expressed such toleration, in which some national constitutions could have included an appeal to God and religion, or an *invocatio dei*, and others could have defined neutrality as laicity, by adopting something close to the formula adopted by postcommunist Poland, which allowed both traditions. Instead the European constitution was drafted so as to ignore God.

This was also a turning away from the European historical tradition. Robert Cooper suggested that modern Europe and the nonsovereign ideal survived because of a particular religious tradition. "Uniquely, the Christian empire of Western Europe divided itself into a spiritual component and a temporal component. The temporal empire ceased to be meaningful in the early Middle Ages, but the spiritual component survived, and while it did do so it prevented the emergence of independent sovereign nation-states."[163] It was exactly this tradition, however, that eroded quickly during the massive wave of secularization in the second half of the twentieth century that accompanied European integration.

Forty years later, both parts of Harold Macmillan's extreme statement that de Gaulle was remaking the Holy Roman Empire while Britain was restoring Rome sounds like nothing more than a very bad joke. Britain (or at least some Britons) may have wanted a version of Rome under Queen Victoria, but by the 1960s it should have been (and actually was) clear to Macmillan that Britain's future was not very imperial. De Gaulle, a Catholic who apparently lacked any deep belief, might have been just as skeptical about the Holy Roman Empire in a continent in which the beginnings of a very rapid secularization were already clearly noticeable. Yet the European project in the 1950s did have a whiff of the Holy Roman Empire about it. Many modern analysts do not like to see this, and have reduced European integration (even in the early phases) to a sort of functionalist consequence of the need to overcome problems in politically significant industries such as coal and steel, as well as agriculture, which could not any longer be well dealt with on a purely national level. At the level of symbolism, however, the European leaders of the time thought quite differently. Why was the treaty establishing the European Economic Community signed in Rome? The Italian capital carried the legacy of two separate but intertwined historical legacies: that of the Roman empire, which had recently been the subject of a misguided and destructive attempt to resurrect it for the twentieth century under Benito Mussolini; and that of the Roman Church.

There are other hints at the symbolism: the adoption of a blue flag with twelve golden stars for the Council of Europe, although at the time of its foundation in May 1949 the Council of Europe had ten members (and the European Coal and Steel Community, the antecedent of the EEC, later had six founding members). Many believed that the twelve stars were a reference to the Book of Revelation, in which a woman is described: "And a great sign was seen in heaven: a woman arrayed with the sun, and the moon under her feet, and upon her head a crown of twelve stars" (Rev. 12: 1). In the Catholic tradition, accurately presented in the stained glass of Strasbourg cathedral, the woman of Revelation was Our Lady, the Mother of God.

The idea of a Catholic Europe had previously been revived at the same time the modern concept of the nation-state emerged. Its advocates presented it as an alternative to the radical rhetoric of revolutionary France, and the vision survived as a constantly underlying alternative in moments of crisis: such as in the aftermath of the French Revolution, or during the era of European fascism. In other words, it surfaced at exactly the same time as did the European alternatives to the nation-state and the Enlightenment secular tradition of popular sovereignty. In 1799 the German poet Novalis, never quite removed from the brink of insanity, produced a pamphlet, "Die Christenheit oder Europa." After a highly romantic evocation of the unity and peace of medieval Christianity, he argued that Christianity would once more pour out its horn of blessing over the peoples. The anarchy of the French Revolution was "the generator of religion."

Blood will stream over Europe until the nations are aware of the terrible madness that drives them in circles: then, pacified by holy music, they will tread before the former altars in their colorful multiplicity and celebrate a feast of love with hot tears in front of the smoking shrines. . . . From the holy lap of a venerable European Council Christianity will be resurrected and the business of religious renewal will be conducted according to an all-encompassing divine plan. No one will any longer protest against Christian or worldly compulsion, for the character of the church will be true freedom, and all necessary reforms will be carried out under its direction as peaceful and formal processes of state.[164]

After World War II, a similar idea drove European integration. According to this concept, a revived Christianity offered an alternative to the failed traditions of the nation-state. The politicians who are sometimes cynically referred to as the "saints" of European integration—Konrad Adenauer, Alcide de Gasperi, Robert Schuman—came from border regions that had a problematical relationship with the nation-state. Adenauer as Mayor of Cologne after World War I had flirted with Rhineland separatism, Schuman was a Lorrainer, and de Gasperi had grown up in the Habsburg empire and had written his doctorate in Vienna. They all thought that the social doctrine of the Catholic church, as stated in Leo XIII's encyclical *Rerum Novarum*, was a better guide to twentieth-century politics than the secular debates of the nation-state. Even socialists, such as the original theorist of imperialism, Rudolf Hilferding, began to argue that the church was the major counterpole to the state and its tradition of violence. All looked back on a Roman ideal: Hilferding even began his final exploration of "Das historische Problem," written under tragic conditions in Vichy France, with the observation that the circumstances of Europe wracked by war were "comparable to those that brought about the fall of the Roman world."[165] And when the new Europe was made, it had to be made through a treaty signed in Rome (March 25, 1957).

The aftermath of September 11, 2001, provided another crisis in that two leading modes of thinking in modern Europe clashed dramatically: on the one hand, the principle of secular liberalism, and its embodiment in the philosophy of the state; and on the other, the idea of plurality and multiculturalism. The terrorist outrages in New York and Washington were motivated by an appeal to fundamental religious values; and did not the principle of multicultural toleration demand respect for such values? It then took a trivial rather than a tragic event to bring home to Europe that the new conflict ran right through the center of European thinking. A few weeks after September 11, on October 6, the Algerian football team played France in Paris, at the Stade de France, for the first time since Algerian independence. As the loudspeakers played the "Marseillaise," young French citizens of North African descent and Islamic faith booed the Republic's anthem and the president of the Republic, Jacques Chirac. The French parliament then rushed to pass legislation making it an offense to mock the "Marseillaise."

There were more severe shocks to come: especially in the country which had been widely held up as the model of toleration and the overcoming of religious divisions from the European past. The Dutch revolt in the sixteenth century had been a revolt of Protestants against the Catholic Spanish monarchy, but the modern history of the Netherlands is the story of the successful integration of the large Catholic community into Dutch politics. A populist political figure, openly gay, who based a large part of his anti-immigrant campaign on the argument that Muslims were intolerant of nontraditional expressions of sexuality, Pim Fortuyn, first built up a major political movement. It was fundamentally a libertarian agenda that drove him to conclude, "This is a full country. . . . I think 16 million Dutchmen are about enough." He was assassinated (by a white radical) in May 2002. In 2004, a filmmaker, Theo van Gogh, who had used verses of the Koran projected onto the bodies of naked women to suggest that Islam oppressed women, was also murdered.

Taking religion seriously now meant that a simple multicultural line about promiscuously accepting all alternatives looked profoundly flawed. Not all "religious" motivations or forms of activity are equally tolerable or acceptable. Some manifestations of religious sensibility are harmful and dangerous, and destroy civic order. To treat this question seriously, however, and to distinguish false from true religion, it became important to think of the way in which the major traditions of the Abrahamic faiths approached the question of religious truth.

The most striking sign of an incipient reorientation of the European religious perspective came in the aftermath of the Iraq controversy, when a number of leading European secular liberal figures came to the conclusion that some positions that they felt to be strongly and distinctively European could not be held or defended on the basis of secular liberal rationality alone. What might be the basis for a legitimate opposition to the Iraq war, which after all could very easily be justified on the grounds of the terrible inhumanity of the Saddam Hussein regime and in particular its genocidal attacks on Shiite Muslims and Kurds? Or how could worries about genetic engineering and DNA manipulation be explained, as these looked like a simple and classic case of the scientific progress that the Enlightenment had always welcomed? Some commentators such as Dominique Moisi and Bernard-Henri Lévy saw in the unique cross-religious grief on the death of Pope John Paul II the beginning of a new European or even global solidarity of responsibility.[166] The mass mourning that followed April 2, 2005, had a greater coherence than the mass antiwar demonstrations of February 15, 2003.

Habermas started to argue that religious and secular language needed to be translated into the other's terms to preserve what he called "normative content" in a world in which the United States was threatening the norms:

> The translation of the godlikeness of humans in the equal and imperative dignity of all humans is an example of such a saving translation. It opens up to a general audience of unbelievers and different believers the content of biblical principles that before were limited to the boundaries of a religious community.

There was a remarkable embrace at the beginning of 2004, when Cardinal Joseph Ratzinger (later to become Pope Benedict XVI), then the prefect of the Vatican's Congregation of the Faith and thus in practice the successor to the Roman Inquisition, held a dialogue in the Munich Katholische Akademie with Habermas. Ratzinger was a great admirer of a previous Inquisitor, Cardinal Lambertini who, as Pope Benedict XIV, had maintained an extensive correspondence with Voltaire, the embodiment of the Enlightenment; and the discussion seemed to conjure up those shades of French Enlightenment thought. Ratzinger concluded that there was a "necessary corelationship of reason and belief, which are called to mutual healing and cleansing, and each of which need each other." He also posed the problem in a fundamental way: that both secular rationality and traditional Christianity had been accustomed to think of themselves as universalistic, but it was very obvious that this claim to universality was contested. "Inter-culturality seems to me today to be an inescapable dimension for the debate about the foundation of humanity, which cannot simply be conducted within the Christian faith or within the traditions of Western rationality. Both consider themselves to be universal, but they must recognize de facto that they are only accepted by parts of humanity, and are only intelligible to parts of humanity." He concluded that it was necessary to reject not only religious pathologies, but also rationalistic pathologies, if the two traditions were to establish a "polyphonic correlationship" and begin a "process of cleansing."[167]

If the United States is an empire in denial, as Niall Ferguson has neatly (but misleadingly) termed it, the European Union is the Holy Roman Empire in denial. The point made by Lambertini's correspondent, Voltaire, that the Holy Roman Empire was not Roman, not an empire, and not holy, might be still more apposite in reference to the European Union. Even in denial, it represents a continuation, long drawn out through time and tradition, of the alternative to cycles of empire-building, overstretch, reactions against imperialism, and the long story of imperial decline and disintegration.

Conclusion

Social processes are characterized by a constant and dynamic instability that increases with the number of interactions involved. A self-contained village may be imagined to be relatively stable (at least in romantic fantasies about the world that is passed)—but when economic and political processes connect billions in a globalized world, we should expect unpredictability. Nevertheless we continue looking for imaginative ways of understanding the world as a whole.

The principal argument of this book is that there is a continual contest between two ways of seeing the world—as a system of rules, or as a series of exercises or applications of power. Globalization fundamentally depends on an acceptance of the legitimacy of rules, but that legitimacy is challenged: in particular when inequalities develop (as they do in the course of globalization), and when even small-scale conflicts polarize the international community (as also occurs frequently in globalization episodes). The result is a continual oscillation between internationalization and pacification on the one hand, and between violence and the breakdown of international and domestic order on the other hand. There are waves of globalization and deglobalization. A similar logic of development had already been presented by Adam Smith and Edward Gibbon in 1776. Smith and Gibbon in their turn used the analogy of ancient Rome as a way of examining the issues at stake between Britain and its North American colonies.

The Roman analogy exerts a powerful attraction. Both those who look for order, and those who criticize order, like to understand modern power systems in terms of a comparison with Rome. The comparison and the lessons were quite systematically expounded in the eighteenth century by Gibbon and Smith, at a moment when the extension and expansion of British imperial rule raised the question of power and rules in a global system of networks. Their reflections on this issue may in a very stylized way be summarized as follows.

First, for the commercial system, Gibbon and Smith saw a historical evolution that involved increasing and widespread prosperity and also a rise in inequality. This was a feature of the world around them, as indeed it is of our own world today; and the authors of 1776 saw the Roman precedent. In an unequal world in which there is also more information available, and people make constant comparisons of each other's wealth and income, they start to look for a rationale and a guide to what is the most appropriate distribution of wealth and scarce resources. The search raises obviously uncomfortable issues, particularly if the focus is on income and prosperity: is it right to object to greater prosperity, which raises even the position of the poor, just because the process also makes for greater inequality? What vision of man's potential and man's proper role is weakened or undermined by such a flourishing of commercial society? A more mundane social historian than Gibbon or Smith would simply leave it at this, and conclude with a simple argument that the Roman empire, and perhaps other imperial systems, foundered because of inequality, and the social revolts that this produced. See you on the barricades, Spartacus.

Second, the eighteenth-century analysts went further in their analysis than simply pointing out that inequality leads to discontent, rebellion, and political disintegration. They were concerned with the rationale that provided a necessary base for imperial rule. As a system of ideas, Gibbon and Smith identified the Roman trajectory as a transition from polytheism (which we translate loosely into the modern analogy of multiculturalism) to monotheism, the imposition of a single set of values and beliefs. Polytheism was originally a way of holding together a vast diversity of cultures, and offered considerable room for toleration. There was room for imperial direction, but not for an imposition of an imperial will. It is hard in this system to derive good rules for the interaction of all the parts of the political and social order.

The two sets of problems for the political order interact: the more people are worried about inequality, the more they demand clear rules about what distribution of property is right, and the more they find the idea of mutual toleration of various and different lifestyles immoral and repulsive. The demand can produce a single ideology (in the Roman case, the rise of Christianity). It can also produce a demand for a single source of order to deal with the threats of violence, that emerge especially in the periphery of the empire.

The rule-based order is strained when it has to deal with inequality, and also when it has to deal with rapid change. The two challenges are likely to come in combination with each other. Dealing with both questions requires constant regulatory and rule-making innovation, in the course of which rules are likely to become more complex, less transparent, and thus more open to the charge of masking concrete and particular interests. In reality, most attempts to produce rules for global order are messy, they are often quite specific, and they are very complex.

The result is to produce a suspicion of the international order, which increases with more international contacts. Such insular hostility is a feature of modern American attitudes to the rest of the world that is often commented on, almost always adversely. Liberal and European critics ask how a great people can be so provincial and inward looking. Yet it is striking that suspicion of internationalism is growing even in the tolerant European Union, which conceives of itself as the opposite of a traditional empire and at the same time runs into the classic problem of how to define a set of values that guide the rules of interaction. As economic and social problems increase, so does skepticism about the European experiment.

The complexity, messiness, and untransparent character of the international order generates conflicts, and conflicts increase the proclivity to see issues in the terms of power and arbitrariness rather than of rules. This can become a vicious cycle, the last stages of which Gibbon detailed with frightening logic. The result is weak and uncertain regimes, which lack legitimacy, and are continually threatened and overwhelmed by external opponents of order.

There are many signs that now we are at the beginning of a new era, in which the "globalization thesis" is being rolled back once more. In the new world, differences become important. Business leaders focus on the way in which they have "traditionally" done business. Individuals see risks coming from the outside rather than opportunities. Citizens detect corruption. Countries are willing to fight trade and currency wars, and to resist external interventions in corporate affairs. Political leaders focus on redesigning the trading and monetary system in order to alter the balance of political and economic power. In this world, conflict tends to escalate and destroys the basis of prosperity and international order. Its inhabitants think about Mars, not Mercury, and work themselves into their own Roman predicament: when rules lose their legitimacy and when violence becomes the counterbalance to power.

It might seem easy to prescribe a remedy for the predicament, and many people certainly wish that there were a patent solution. There is certainly an ideal: rules are needed in the international system, as in the domestic order. Strong international rules make it easier to apply strong domestic rules, and vice versa. The rules need to be coherent, intelligible, clear, and above all universal and generalizable—in other words, not applied to specific groups or interests. This is, in short, the perennial dream of classical (i.e., Smithian) liberalism, or liberalism in the European rather than the American meaning of the term.

It might help to treat the perpetual search for rule and legitimacy on two different levels, and not to assume that they are quite simply dependent on each other. The first level concerns the appropriate regulation of a commercial order; the second the demand for a peaceful order.

The most obvious (but also obviously utopian) Smithian step today would be a very simple one: the complete elimination of restraints on international trade. The end of tariffs would mean the obsolescence of the complex struggles on interpretation of rules of origin, or about why Europeans should give preferences to bananas produced by African, Caribbean, and Pacific countries. Simplicity and transparency make for greater legitimacy of rules, and free trade is as simple and as general a rule as could be desired. Such a solution would be desirable on two grounds: in domestic relations, it would eliminate a large part of the potential for rent-seeking and corruption in which particular interests use the political process to extract concessions and benefits. Secondly, in international relations, it would remove a source of conflict. While the increased legalization of international trade and of corporate governance over the past twenty years breeds conflicts and tends to escalate in a clash of jurisdictions, a very general adoption of a principle could be a way of removing harmful conflicts. Better and simpler domestic and international rules would complement each other. The Smithian answer would also deal with the vulnerability of the current international order as described in chapter 3: that the large-scale elimination of rules about money and the intensification of rules about trade make for a backlash against trade when popular discontent turns against internationalism.

There are nevertheless many obvious and practical objections about the transition costs while such a move to global free trade occurs, and there are certainly numerous examples in the world today of uncertainties caused by the reduction of old trade barriers. Central American or Bangladeshi textile producers have been sharply affected by the move to free the textile regime of quotas, and thus to allow more East Asian (largely Chinese) products onto the markets of industrial countries. Such cases would require a substantial amount of support while the transition to the new and better regime is underway: perhaps fiscal incentives for industries to diversify, or the extension of social safety nets to those who lose their livelihoods. They do not however, present an insuperable barrier to the idea of a radical liberalization.

World free trade would reduce but not eliminate the need for regulation of business. Such regulation is also likely to be complicated, and different patterns of regulation, reflecting different national interest constellations, are bound to clash. So the problem of complex rules and the resentment they produce returns.

The liberal commercial solution on its own is not sufficient, particularly if its advocates insist on thinking that it necessarily and by itself provides an overall framework for building a civilized society. The current liberal order is also unstable and vulnerable to backlash because its major players are obsessed with processes. The most common view of the world is that processes create order. Europeans thus frequently claim that the cooperative behavior established by first the European Coal and Steel Community, then the European Economic Community, then the European Community, and then the European Union launched a functionalist snowball, in which the partners were bound ever more closely together as their interactions and their interdependence increased.

Scarred by World War II, Europeans had decided that economic interaction could produce common interests and thus peace. This was a regional version of the old liberal internationalist argument that commerce makes for peace as well as prosperity. It is attractive to beat swords into plowshares. Yet it would be a mistake to leap to the conclusion that if we become very efficient and successful at making plowshares, this will automatically eliminate swords.

Discussions of international order based on the prevalent functional-ist logic ignore the ethical foundations that are needed to build legiti-macy in the longer run. There is a limit to the extent that the demand for good politics can be satisfied by debates about which countries should be given permanent seats on the United Nations Security Council, or be represented in the G-7, G-8, or G-9; or whether voting in the European Union should be determined by the Treaty of Nice or alternately by the 2004 constitutional treaty. The procedural or architectural debates side-step the major issues and frequently make for harsher conflicts. Practical experience demonstrates that some common agreement on basic princi-ples is a prerequisite for setting successful agendas in international meetings. Debates that are solely confined to process tend to increase mistrust: Is the agenda being manipulated? Is the other side using unfair negotiating tactics, or are they simply (and unfairly) more clever?

Looking at past instances, the most successful examples of benign hegemony involved the elaboration of values that drew other and dif-ferent societies into a peaceful order. Peace is a value, and it does not emerge simply out of processes. Ancient Rome found the formulation of such a vision completely impossible: and so does any order that thinks of itself as imperial. The European problem, as analyzed in chap-ter 7, lies in the confusion of reverence for process with reverence for some higher goal, which cannot be easily formulated. The Oxford philosopher Isaiah Berlin pointed out the problem in a remarkable essay on "European Unity and Its Vicissitudes" in 1959. Berlin saw a re-version to a Europe that was universal in that it rejected the celebration of the particular and the different in late-eighteenth-century Romanti-cism. Before that era, the world was "a single, intelligible whole. It con-sisted of certain stable ingredients, material and spiritual; if they were not stable they were not real." After the catastrophes of the mid-twentieth century, which could not as easily be overcome politically or psychologically as they were materially (in the age of the Marshall Plan), there was a need for a new vision: "there is a return to the ancient notion of natural law, but for some of us, in empiricist dress—no longer necessarily based on theological or metaphysical foundations."[168]

As Berlin noticed, the eighteenth-century thinkers saw this problem very clearly. Smith was acutely aware of the necessity of formulating what he called "general rules of morality." They were derived from experience: "experience of what, in particular instances, our moral faculties, our natural sense of merit and propriety, approve or disapprove of." Such general rules of conduct "when they have been fixed in our mind by habitual reflection, are of great use in correcting the misrepresentations of self-love concerning what is fit and proper to be done in our present situation." This code provided a natural law framework for human legislation. It existed as a primary given.

> Human society would crumble into nothing if mankind were not generally impressed with a reverence for those important rules of conduct. The reverence is still further enhanced by an opinion which is first impressed by nature, and afterwards confirmed by reasoning and philosophy, that those important rules of morality are the commands and laws of the Deity, who will finally reward the obedient, and punish the transgressors of their duty.[169]

Another way of formulating the Roman dilemma then is to ask how to deal with a basic human proclivity for violence. The most obvious answer is that in the process of civilization, law (or, in other words, a system of rules) is needed to restrain violence. Ancient Rome actually found it almost impossible to engage in a systematic elaboration of the fundaments of rule and law. The basic model is given in the Abrahamic faiths by the Ten Commandments. But the Commandments are derived from God, not from an argument about pragmatic necessity, or a case derived from the functional logic of increased interaction and communication.

It is important to note that this kind of interpretation leaves little room for the vision made famous by Samuel Huntington. The "clash of civilizations" is another version of the non-globalization mindset explored in this book, but it is a peculiar one that has a mixed pedigree. The notion of an inevitable conflict between an Islamic (or an Asian) vision and a Western one is based on two kinds of argument: first, about inevitable and ineradicable cultural differences; and second, about the impact of economic and social modernization on non-Western traditional societies. In the clash of civilizations a widespread rejection of Western models of modernization follows as a backlash produced by *ressentiment* generated after the breakdown of traditional order. Ideologues then create and manipulate an idealized vision of the past to counter the despiritualizing secular progress; but this anti-Western reaction is very frequently cast in terms themselves borrowed from the

West. This is the phenomenon that Ian Buruma and Avishai Margalit have in a different context dubbed "occidentalism": the desire to overthrow and overcome Western modernity or "rootless, arrogant, greedy, decadent, frivolous cosmopolitanism."[170]

Depending on which of the above analyses are preferred, different solutions are held out. If cultural differences are really so profound, then imperial conflict and conquest is the only adequate answer. If, on the other hand, the problem lies in discontents about modernity, and poverty and marginality are the breeding grounds for violence and terrorism, then a better and more socially egalitarian modernization can hold a more effective cure. Much contemporary debate, especially after September 11, 2001, fluctuates between these poles. Should we fight or buy off the barbarians at the gate? Yet both options look like different aspects of the old but unsatisfactory Roman solution: conquer and provide prosperity. There is only a difference in emphasis. The first is arrogantly belligerent and the second arrogantly patronizing. Both recommend more power and more modernization.

There is a fundamental as well as a fundamentalist objection, however, to more modernization (or more globalization) as a simple answer. In the second half of the twentieth century, a powerful modernization paradigm had become a way of explaining the necessity of progress and development. It was based very explicitly on a means-rational argument. Development was presented by its advocates as a good in itself that would be automatically seen as a good by any intelligent observer. It was not usually seen as linked to any higher value, any way of achieving greater human dignity or freedom. Instead, it was a technocratic mill through which humanity was supposed to be minced in the cause of advance and prosperity. And it was exactly the technocratic vision of modernization that produced as a response a new anti-Western sentiment that claimed to be more profound and more spiritual than a superficial materialism, while at the same time holding out nationally defined styles of capitalism.

There exists an alternative to the challenge and response model that has as its outcome the clash of civilizations. The other path depends on dialogue within a shared natural law framework. Instead of thinking that technical development will automatically produce prosperity and thus solve, as it were, by a kind of magic the problem of values, we need to think and talk explicitly about values. We will identify more commonalities across cultures in this discussion than we initially might have supposed. A symbolic and perhaps important exemplification of unity around values was the line-up in modern Rome at the funeral of Pope John Paul II, the best-attended funeral in the history of the world. Christian, Jewish, and Muslim leaders appeared in a show of unity, and where the President of Israel shook hands with the President of Iran. The *Financial Times* commented, "There has been little like it since eight crowned heads of Europe assembled for the funeral of Britain's King Edward VII in 1910."[171]

A notion of the commonality of values despite difference might even be extended beyond the brackets linking different religious traditions. The kind of dialogue between apparently rival traditions of thinking—exemplified in the debate between Jürgen Habermas and Cardinal Ratzinger—offers a way to provide a universal basis for restraining violence that is independent of the chance and necessarily unsatisfactory results of process and procedure. It does not depend on a simple functionalist logic. Our debate must avoid the non–value-based escapism of simply technocratic solutions, and it needs to concern itself with fundamental values.

Notes

1. Helen Milner, *Interests, Institutions and Information: Domestic Politics and International Relations* (Princeton: Princeton University Press, 1997), 244.

2. Robert O. Keohane, *After Hegemony: Cooperation and Discord in the World Political Economy* (Princeton: Princeton University Press, 1984); G. John Ikenberry, *After Victory: Institutions, Strategic Restraint, and the Rebuilding of Order after Major Wars* (Princeton: Princeton University Press, 2001); John J. Mearsheimer, *The Tragedy of Great Power Politics* (New York: Norton, 2003).

3. Gibbon to Adam Ferguson, April 1, 1776, in *The Letters of Edward Gibbon*, edited by J. E. Norton, Vol. 2 (New York: Macmillan, 1956), 101.

4. The editions cited in this book are Adam Smith, *An Inquiry into the Nature and Causes of the Wealth of Nations*, edited by Edwin Cannan, with a new Preface by George J. Stigler (Chicago: University of Chicago Press, 1976); and Edward Gibbon, *The Decline and Fall of the Roman Empire*, 3 vols. (New York: Modern Library, 1983).

5. *Edward Gibbon: bicentenary essays*, edited by David Womersley, with the assistance of John Burrow and John Pocock (Oxford: Voltaire Foundation, 1997); David Womersley, *The Transformation of "The Decline and Fall of the Roman Empire"* (Cambridge and New York: Cambridge University Press, 1988).

6. Edward Gibbon, *Memoirs of My Life*, edited by Betty Radice (Harmondsworth: Penguin, 1984), 16; see also p. 143 for an alternative formulation.

7. Gibbon to Richard Hurd, Ca. August 1772, *Letters of Edward Gibbon*, I: 329.

8. Gibbon to Deyverdun, May 7, 1776; and May 20, 1783, *Letters of Edward Gibbon*, II: 104.

9. Patricia B. Craddock, *Edward Gibbon: Luminous Historian, 1772–1794*, (Baltimore: Johns Hopkins University Press, 1989), 50.

10. Gibbon to John Whitaker, October 16, 1775, *Letters of Edward Gibbon*, II: 90.

11. Gibbon, *Decline and Fall*, I: 453.

12. Craddock, *Gibbon*, 170.

13. Gibbon, *Decline and Fall*, I: 1–2. Citations in the following passages refer to this edition, and page numbers appear in parentheses.

14. Roy Porter, *Edward Gibbon: Making history* (London: Weidenfeld and Nicolson, 1988), 147.

15. Gibbon, *Memoirs*, 122–33.

16. J.G.A. Pocock, "Between Machiavelli and Hume: Gibbon as Civic Humanist and Philosophical Historian," in *Edward Gibbon and the Decline and Fall of the Roman Empire*, edited by G. W. Bowersock, John Clive, and Stephen R. Graubard (Cambridge: Harvard University Press, 1977), 112.

17. J.G.A. Pocock, "Gibbon and the Late Enlightenment," in *Virtue, Commerce, and History: Essays on Political Thought and History, Chiefly in the Eighteenth Century* (Cambridge: Cambridge University Press, 1985), 149.

18. Political Economy Club, *Revised Report of the Proceedings at the Dinner of 31 May 1876 Held in Celebration of the Hundredth Year of the Publication of the "Wealth of Nations"* (London: Longmans Green, 1876), 47.

19. Alexander Cairncross, "The Market and the State", in *The Market and the State: Essays in Honour of Adam Smith*, edited by Thomas Wilson and Andrew S. Skinner (Oxford: Oxford University Press, 1976), 134; proceedings of a conference at the University of Glasgow, April 1976.

20. Smith, *Wealth of Nations*, II: 284. Citations in the following passages refer to this edition, and page numbers appear in parentheses.

21. Gibbon, *Memoirs*, 78.

22. See E. A. Wrigley, *Continuity, Chance and Change: the Character of the Industrial Revolution in England* (Cambridge: Cambridge University Press, 1988), 57–60.

23. Adam Smith, with an introduction by E. G. West, *The Theory of the Moral Sentiments* (Indianapolis: Liberty Classics, 1976), 264–65.

24. Quoted in Joseph Frank, *Dostoevsky: The Mantle of the Prophet 1871–1881* (Princeton: Princeton University Press, 2002), 288.

25. On this, see Garth Fowden, *Empire to Commonwealth: Consequences of Monotheism in Late Antiquity* (Princeton: Princeton University Press, 1993).

26. Michael Gorbachev, *Gipfelgespräche: Geheime Protokolle aus meiner Amtszeit* (Berlin: Rowohlt, 1993), 128–29.

27. Quoted in Alastair Horne, *Macmillan, Volume II, 1957–1986* (London: Macmillan, 1989), 284.

28. There is an extensive literature on the "democratic peace," taking up an idea originally propounded by Kant. See Michael Doyle, "Kant, Liberal Legacies and Foreign Affairs," *Philosophy and Public Affairs* 12 (1983): 205–35, 323–53; and "Liberalism and World Politics" *American Political Science Review* 80

(1986): 1151–69. See also Bruce Russett, *Grasping the Democratic Peace: Principles for a Post–Cold War World* (Princeton: Princeton University Press, 1993).

29. Wilfrid Ward, ed. *Newman's "Apologia pro vita sua"* (London: Oxford University Press, 1913), 336–37.

30. Norman Angell, *The Great Illusion: A Study of the Relation of Military Power to National Advantage* (Toronto: McClelland and Goodchild, 1913), 271.

31. Notably in William Appleman Williams, *Empire as a Way of Life: An Essay on the Causes and Character of America's Present Predicament, along with a few thoughts about an alternative* (New York: Oxford University Press, 1980).

32. The very generalized use of "empire" and "imperialism" as a way of understanding the modern world was presented in what became a cult book by Michael Hardt and Toni Negri, *Empire* (Cambridge: Harvard University Press, 2000). The recent books include Chalmers Johnson, *The Sorrows of Empire: Militarism, Secrecy, and the End of the Republic* (New York: Metropolitan, 2004); Benjamin R. Barber, *Fear's Empire: War, Terrorism, and Democracy* (New York: Norton, 2003); Michael Mann, *Incoherent Empire* (New York: Verso, 2003); Emmanuel Todd, *After the Empire: The Breakdown of the American Order* (New York: Columbia University Press, 2003).

33. Charles A. Beard, *Giddy Minds and Foreign Quarrels: An Estimate of American Foreign Policy* (New York: Macmillan, 1939), 65, 78, 81–2. Also Andrew J. Bacevich, *American Empire: The Realities and Consequences of U.S. Diplomacy* (Cambridge: Harvard University Press, 2002), 11–23, 242–43.

34. Niall Ferguson, *Empire: The Rise and Demise of the British World Order and the Lessons for Global Power* (New York: Basic, 2003), 367.

35. Michael Ignatieff, *Empire Lite: Nation-building in Bosnia, Kosovo, and Afghanistan* (London: Vintage, 2003).

36. *Washington Post*, December 28, 2003.

37. See his review of a recent collection of this literature: G. John Ikenberry, "Illusions of Empire: Defining the New American Order," *Foreign Affairs*, March/April 2004.

38. See Charles Kindleberger, *The World in Depression, 1929–1939* (London: Allen Lane, 1973); Robert Gilpin, *The Political Economy of International Relations* (Princeton: Princeton University Press, 1987).

39. Charles P. Kindleberger, "Rules vs. Men: Lessons from a Century of Monetary Policy", in *Zerrissene Zwischenkriegszeit: wirtschaftshistorische Beiträge: Knut Borchardt zum 65. Geburtstag* edited by Christoph Buchheim, Michael Hutter, Harold James (Baden-Baden: Nomos, 1994), 175.

40. Gilpin, *Political Economy*, 78. See also Aaron Friedberg's reflection on a past experience of hegemonic weariness: *The Weary Titan: Britain and the Ex-*

perience of Relative Decline, 1895–1905 (Princeton: N.J.: Princeton University Press, 1988).

41. See for instance, Harold James, "From Grandmotherliness to Governance: The Development of IMF Conditionality," in *Finance and Development*, December 1998.

42. Robert Kagan, *Of Paradise and Power: America and Europe in the New World Order* (New York: Knopf, 2003).

43. Hans J. Morgenthau, *Politics among Nations: The Struggle for Power and Peace*, 3rd ed. (New York: Knopf, 1963), 63.

44. *Financial Times*, "Ukraine Poll Divides EU and Russia," November 28, 2004.

45. F. A. Hayek, *The Constitution of Liberty* (London: Routledge and Hegan Paul, 1960), 226.

46. Friedrich Hayek, *The Road to Serfdom* (London: Routledge, 1944), 163.

47. Gibbon, *Decline and Fall*, II: 728.

48. See Philip H. Gordon and Sophie Meunier, *The French Challenge: Adapting to Globalization* (Washington, D.C.: Brookings Institution Press, 2001).

49. See Keohane, *After Hegemony*.

50. Julius W. Pratt, *Cordell Hull, 1933–44* (New York: Cooper Square, 1964), 112.

51. Address by Henry Morgenthau, Jr., July 1, 1944, *United Nations Monetary and Financial Conference, Bretton Woods, New Hampshire: Final Act and Related Documents* (Washington, D.C.: Government Printing House, 1944).

52. See Charles Lipson, *Standing Ground: Protecting Foreign Capital in the Nineteenth and Twentieth Centuries* (Berkeley: University of California Press, 1985).

53. Friedrich List, *The National System of Political Economy*, transl. Sampson S. Lloyd (Fairfield, N.J.: Kelley, 1991), 368.

54. See the hostile account by Henri Hauser, *Germany's Commercial Grip on the World, Her Business Methods Explained* (London: Eveleigh Nash, 1917).

55. E. E. Schattschneider, *Politics, Pressures and the Tariff: A Study of Free Private Enterprise in Pressure Politics, as Shown in the 1929–1930 Revision of the Tariff* (New York: Prentice-Hall, 1935); Mancur Olson, Jr., *The logic of Collective Action: Public Goods and the Theory of Groups* (Cambridge: Harvard University Press, 1965).

56. See the model of this process described by Kyle Bagwell and Robert W. Staiger, *The Economics of the World Trading System* (Cambridge: MIT Press, 2002).

57. Kenneth Dam, *The Rules of the Global Game: A New Look at U.S. International Economic Policymaking* (Chicago: University of Chicago Press, 2001), 119.

58. See Fritz Breuss, Stefan Griller, Erich Vranes, eds., *The Banana Dispute: An Economic and Legal Analysis* (Vienna and New York: Springer, 2003); Karen Alter and Sophie Meunier, "Nested and Overlapping Regimes in the Transatlantic Banana Dispute," working paper, 2004; also Gordon and Meunier, *The French Challenge.*

59. Robert J. Samuelson, "The Airbus Showdown," *Newsweek*, December 13, 2004.

60. See Carmen Reinhart and Kenneth Rogoff, NBER Working Paper 10296, "Serial Default and the 'Paradox' of Rich to Poor Capital Flows," February 2004.

61. See Niall Ferguson, *The House of Rothschild: Money's Prophets 1798–1848* (New York: Viking, 1998), 231–56.

62. Max Huber, quoted in Independent Commission of Experts, *Switzerland National Socialism and the Second World War* (Zurich: Pendo, 2002), 299. I have added the word "unconditonally" from the German original "selbstverständlich, dass das Unternehmen seine volkswirtschaftliche Aufgabe in jedem Lande, desses Staat ihm Aufnahme und dessen recht ihm Schutz gewährt, in unbedingter Loyalität und mit dem Willen zu verständnisvoller Einordnung erfülle."

63. Quoted in Henry A. Turner, *General Motors and the Nazis* (New Haven: Yale University Press, 2005), 27.

64. "Betriebsklima: Küssen verboten! Wal-Mart untersagt den Mitarbeiten die Liebe zu Kollegen," *Stern* 13, March 23, 2005, pp. 58–59.

65. See Wendy Dobson and Pierre Jacquet, *Financial Services Liberalization in the WTO* (Washington, D.C.: Institute for International Economics, 1998), 29.

66. See Dam, *Rules of the Global Game*, 228.

67. "For Citigroup, Scandal in Japan Shows Danger of Global Sprawl," *Wall Street Journal*, December 22, 2004.

68. See Joseph Weiler, "The Constitution of the Common Market Place: The Free Movement of Goods," in *The Evolution of EU Law*, edited by P. P. Craig and G. de Bùrca (New York: Oxford University Press, 1999).

69. "Indonesia-Memorandum of Economic and Financial Policies," January 15, 1998; available on www.imf.org.

70. "Russia Looks East as West Disappoints," *Financial Times*, January 3, 2005.

71. See Harold James, *International Monetary Cooperation since Bretton Woods* (New York: Oxford University Press, 1996), 50.

72. See Henry B. Russell, *International Monetary Conferences: Their Purposes, Character, and Results, with a study of the conditions of currency and*

finance in Europe and America during intervening periods, and in their relations to international action (New York and London: Harper, 1898). See also Luca Einaudi, *Money and Politics: European Monetary Unification and the International Gold Standard (1865–1873)* (Oxford and New York: Oxford University Press, 2001).

73. Dam, *Rules of the Game*, 24.

74. Karl Polanyi, *The Great Transformation* (New York: Farrar 1944), 193–94.

75. For a contrary view, see Barry Eichengreen, *Golden Fetters: The Gold Standard and the Great Depression, 1919–1939* (New York: Oxford University Press, 1992), 8: "What rendered the commitment to the gold standard credible, then, was that the commitment was international, not merely national. That commitment was activated through international cooperation." There is a good description of the "increased cooperation" after 1890 in Eichengreen's *Globalizing Capital: A History of the International Monetary System* (Princeton: Princeton University Press, 1996), 32–35.

76. Article IV, Section 1 (a) of International Monetary Fund, Articles of Agreement (1944).

77. Alain Peyrefitte, *C'était de Gaulle* (Paris: Gallimard, 2002), 603, 663.

78. See on this episode James, *International Monetary Cooperation*, 212.

79. Jean Peyrelevade and Jean-Antoine Kosciusko-Morizet, *La mort du dollar* (Paris, 1975), 142.

80. Cited in James, *International Monetary Cooperation*, 298.

81. Smith, *Wealth of Nations*, vol. V, chap. 3, pp. 446, 466–67.

82. The most famous version of this kind of thesis was presented by Paul Kennedy, *The Rise and Fall of the Great Powers: Economic Change and Military Conflict from 1500 to 2000* (New York: Random House, 1987).

83. Dominic Lieven, *Empire* (Cambridge: Harvard University Press, 2000).

84. The classic account of the postwar order is by Richard Gardner, *Sterling-Dollar Diplomacy: The Origins and the Prospects of Our International Economic Order* (New York: McGraw-Hill, 1969). See now G. John Ikenberry, *After Victory: Institutions, Strategic Restraint, and the Rebuilding of Order after Major Wars* (Princeton: Princeton University Press, 2001).

85. Patrick Low, *Trading Free: The GATT and U.S. Trade Policy* (New York: Twentieth Century Fund Press, 1995), 247.

86. See Kenneth Rogoff and Maurice Obstfeld, "The Unsustainable US Current Account Position Revealed," NBER Working Paper 10869, November 2004; Barry Eichengreen, "Global Imbalances and the Lessons of Bretton Woods," NBER Working Paper 10497, May 2004.

87. The argument is most fully laid out in a set of papers by a group of Deutsche Bank economists: Michael P. Dooley, David Folkerts-Landau, Peter Garber, "An Essay on the Revived Bretton Woods System," NBER Working Paper 9971, September 2003; "The Revived Bretton Woods System: The Effects of Periphery Intervention and Reserve Management on Interest Rates and Exchange Rates in Center Countries," NBER Working Paper 10332, March 2004; "Direct Investment, Rising Real Wages and the Absorption of Excess Labor in the Periphery," NBER Working Paper 10626, July 2004; "The US Current Account Deficit and Economic Development: Collateral for a Total Return Swap," NBER Working Paper 10727, September 2004.

88. Eichengreen, "Global Imbalances."

89. See Nouriel Roubini and Brad Setser, "Will the Bretton Woods 2 Regime Unravel Soon? The Risk of a Hard Landing in 2005–6," paper for conference on "The Revived Bretton Woods System: A New Paradigm for Asian Development?" Federal Reserve Bank of San Francisco Conference, February 4, 2005.

90. This is a point made very effectively by Tim Congdon: see Lombard Street Research Ltd., "The Analyses of Unsustainability, and Total Unsustainability, Based on the Familiar Theory of Debt Dynamics Have Been Dumbfounded," *Monthly Economic Review*, November/December 2002, p. 5.

91. Though see Keith Bradsher, *High and Mighty: SUVs—The World's Most Dangerous Vehicles and How They Got That Way* (New York: Public Affairs, 2002).

92. See Paco Underhill, *Call of the Mall* (New York and London: Simon and Schuster, 2004).

93. Joseph S. Nye, *Soft Power: The Means to Success in World Politics* (New York: Public Affairs, 2004).

94. Peyrefitte, *de Gaulle*, 664. See also Francis J. Gavin, *Gold, Dollars, and Power: The Politics of International Monetary Relations, 1958–1968* (Chapel Hill: University of North Carolina Press, 2004), 121.

95. Lawrence Kotlikoff, Hans Fehr and Sabine Jokisch, "The Developed World's Demographic Transition—The Roles of Capital Flows, Immigration, and Policy," mimeo, October 2003; Lawrence Kotlikoff and Niall Ferguson, "Going Critical," *National Interest*, Fall 2003.

96. IMF, *World Economic Outlook*, September 2004, pp. 218–19.

97. Stanley Fischer, "On the Need for an International Lender of Last Resort," *Journal of Economic Perspectives* 13, no. 4 (Fall 1999): 85–104.

98. Gibbon, *Decline and Fall*, I: 440.

99. Joseph A. Schumpeter, *Capitalism, Socialism, and Democracy*, 2nd ed. (New York: Harper, 1947).

100. Smith, *Wealth of Nations* (1976 ed.), I: 445.

101. Edward M. Bernstein, "War and the Pattern of Business Cycles," *American Economic Review* 30 (1940): 24–35.

102. Figures from "In Perspective: America's Conflicts," *New York Times*, April 20, 2003, p. B16.

103. Edward Luttwak, "Toward Post-Heroic Warfare: The Obsolescence of Total War," *Foreign Affairs* 74, no. 3 (May/June 1995); Jeremy Black, *Why Wars Happen* (London: Reaktion Books, 1998); Black, *Warfare and the Western World 1882–1975*, (Bloomington, Ind.: Indiana University Press, 2002).

104. Smith, *Wealth of Nations*, II: 455–56.

105. The canonical texts are J. A. Hobson, *Imperialism: A Study* (New York: J. Pott, 1902); Rudolf Hilferding, *Das Finanzkapital* (Vienna, 1910); V. I. Lenin, *Imperialism: The Highest Stage of Capitalism* [1916], new trans. (New York: International Publishers, 1939). For analyses, see David Fieldhouse, "Imperialism: An Historical Revision," *Economic History Review* 14 (1961); and Wolfgang J. Mommsen, *Imperialismustheorien* (Göttingen: Vandenhoeck und Ruprecht, 1977).

106. Martin Luther, "Trade and Usury," in Walther Brandt, ed., *Luther's Works, Vol. 45: The Christian in Society* (Philadephia: Muhlenberg Press, 1962), 245–46.

107. See Emma Rothschild, *Economic Sentiments: Adam Smith, Condorcet and the Enlightenment* (Cambridge: Harvard University Press, 2001), 27, 32, 73.

108. Smith, *Wealth of Nations*, II: 158.

109. Lucy S. Sutherland, *The East India Company in Eighteenth-Century Politics* (Westport, Conn.: Hyperion, 1979).

110. J. A. Hobson, *Imperialism: A Study* [1902] (Ann Arbor: University of Michigan, 1965), 8.

111. Ibid., 38, 125, 127, 357.

112. Ibid., 201–2, 222.

113. George Friedman and Meredith LeBard, *The Coming War with Japan* (New York: St. Martin's, 1991).

114. Werner Sombart, *Händler und Helden: Patriotische Besinnungen* (Munich and Leipzig: Duncker and Humblot, 1915).

115. Amy Chua, *World on Fire: How Exporting Free Market Democracy Breeds Ethnic Hatred and Global Instability* (New York: Doubleday, 2003).

116. Gibbon, *Decline and Fall*, vol. I, chap. 24, pp. 838–39.

117. Fowden, *Empire to Commonwealth*, 14.

118. Jack Snyder, *Myths of Empire: Domestic Politics and International Ambition* (Ithaca: Cornell University Press, 1991).

119. Quoted in Richard Koebner and Helmut Dan Schmidt, *Imperialism: The Story and Significance of a Political Word, 1840–1960* (Cambridge: Cambridge University Press, 1964), 201; Ferguson, *Empire*, xxiii; Paul Leroy-Beaulieu, *De la colonisation chez les peuples modernes* 6th ed. Paris: Alcan, 1908), xxvii, 687.

120. See Michael W. Doyle, *Empires* (Ithaca: Cornell University Press, 1986).

121. Richard Cobden, *How Wars Are Got Up in India: The Origin of the Burmese War* (London: William and Frederick Cash, 1953), 58.

122. Patrick O'Brien, "European Economic Development: The Contribution of the Periphery," *Economic History Review* 35 (1982): 1–18.

123. P. J. Cain and A. G. Hopkins, "The Political Economy of British Overseas Expansion, 1750–1914," *Economic History Review* 33 (1980): 484–85; Eric Hobsbawm, *Industry and Empire: An Economic History of Britain since 1750* (London: Weidenfeld & Nicolson, 1968), 122.

124. Koebner and Schmidt, *Imperialism*, 123.

125. Benjamin Disraeli, Crystal Palace Speech, June 24, 1872, "Conservative and Liberal Principles," in *Selected Speeches of the Late Right Honourable the Earl of Beaconsfield, arranged and edited with introduction and explanatory notes by T. E. Kebbel*, vol. 2 (London: Longmans, 1882), 530–51.

126. See Ronald Robinson and John Gallagher, with Alice Denny, *Africa and the Victorians: The Official Mind of Imperialism* (London: Macmillan, and New York: St. Martin's, 1961).

127. Peter Marsh, *Joseph Chamberlain: Entrepreneur in Politics* (New Haven: Yale University Press, 1994), 585, 590, 614.

128. Eric Hobsbawm, *The Age of Empire, 1875–1914* (London: Cardinal, 1989), 123.

129. See the recent books by David Anderson, *Histories of the Hanged: The Dirty War in Kenya and the End of Empire* (New York: Norton, 2004); Caroline Elkins, *Imperial Reckoning: The Untold Story of the End of Empire in Kenya* (New York: Henry Holt, 2004).

130. Richard Haas quoted in Andrew J. Bacevich, *American Empire: The Realities and Consequences of U.S. Diplomacy* (Cambridge: Harvard University Press, 2002), 219.

131. See especially Kenneth Waltz, *The Spread of Nuclear Weapons: More May be Better*, (London: International Institute for Strategic Studies, 1981).

132. Jack A. Goldstone et al., *State Failure Task Force Report: Phase III Findings* (McLean, Va: Science Applications International Corporation (SAIC), September 30, 2000).

133. See Paul Collier, *Breaking the Conflict Trap: Civil War and Development Policy* (Washington, D.C.: World Bank, and New York: Oxford University Press, 2003).

134. Stuart Eizenstat, John Edward Porter, and Jeremy Weinstein, "Rebuilding Weak States," *Foreign Affairs*, January/February 2005.

135. For instance, John Lewis Gaddis, "Grand Strategy in the Second Term," *Foreign Affairs*, January/February 2005.

136. Chalmers Johnson, "America's Empire of Bases," TomDispatch.com, January 15, 2004. Also Chalmers Johnson, *Blowback: The Costs and Consequences of American Empire*, (New York: Metropolitan/Owl Book, 2004).

137. Lynne Truss, *Eats, Shoots & Leaves: The Zero Tolerance Approach to Punctuation* (New York: Gotham, 2004).

138. "The National Security Strategy of the United States of America," available at http://www.whitehouse.gov/nsc/nss.html.

139. See especially Jeffrey Kopstein and David A. Reilly, "Geographic Diffusion and the Transformation of the Postcommunist World," *World Politics* 53, no. 1 (October 2000): 1–37.

140. Fareed Zakaria, *The Future of Freedom: Illiberal Democracy at Home and Abroad* (New York: Norton, 2003).

141. Of this group, Leonard is the only European author.

142. Cited in Jean Lacouture, *De Gaulle: The Ruler 1945–1970* (New York: Norton, 1992), 353.

143. Gibbon, *Decline* and Fall, vol. III, chap. 68, p. 784.

144. Montek Singh Ahluwalia, "The Emerging Global Financial Architecture and Its Implications for India," Indian Council for Research in International Economic Relations, paper, July 1999.

145. Richard Layard, *Happiness: Lessons from a New Science* (New York: Penguin, 2005), 164–65.

146. Hans Magnus Enzensberger, "Vom Missvergnügen an der Politik," *Neue Zürcher Zeitung*, January 12, 2005.

147. Friedrich Naumann, *Central Europe* (London: King, 1916), 84.

148. Ibid., 97.

149. Ibid., 129.

150. Ibid., 139, 141.

151. See Harold James, *A German Identity 1770–1990* (London: Weidenfeld, 1989), 158; Jean Monnet, *Memoirs* (London: Collins, 1978), 339.

152. Andrew Moravcsik, "Striking a New Transatlantic Bargain," *Foreign Affairs*, 82, no. 4. (July/August 2003).

153. Robert Cooper, *The Breaking of Nations: Order and Chaos in the Twenty-first Century* (London: Atlantic Monthly Press, 2003), 7, 16, 53.

154. Jeremy Rifkin, *The European Dream* (New York: Penguin, 2003), 231.

155. "Genoa Summit Meeting," *New York Times*, July 21, 2001; "Chirac Takes Aim at EU Liberals," *Guardian*, March 24, 2005.

156. See Anne-Marie Slaughter, *A New World Order* (Princeton: Princeton University Press, 2004), 189.

157. Rifkin, *The European Dream*, 191, 196.

158. Dominique Strauss-Kahn, "Une nation est née," *Le Monde*, February 26, 2004.

159. Jürgen Habermas, "Was bedeutet der Denkmalsturz?" *Frankfurter Allgemeine Zeitung*, April 17, 2003.

160. "Chirac Will Not Resign If Vote Is Lost," *Financial Times*, April 15, 2005.

161. Heinrich Heine quoted in Andrei S. Markovits, *Amerika, dich hasst sich besser: Antiamerikanismus und Antisemitismus in Europa* (Hamburg: Konkret, 2004), 83.

162. See Joseph Weiler, *Ein christliches Europa* (Salzburg: Pustet, 2004).

163. Cooper, *The Breaking of Nations*, 21.

164. Carl Seeling, ed., *Novalis: Gesammelte Werke* (Zurich: Bühl, 1945), 24, 32, 34.

165. Rudolf Hilferding, "Das historische Problem," *Zeitschrift für Politik* 1 (1954): 293–324. (The article was published only posthumously.)

166. Bernard-Henri Lévy, *Wall Street Journal*, April 5, 2005; Dominique Moisi, *Ouest-France*, April 5, 2005.

167. Jürgen Habermas and Joseph Ratzinger, *Dialektik der Säkulisierung: Über Vernunft und Religion* (Freiburg: Herder, 2005), Habermas quote on p. 32, Ratzinger quotes on pp. 53, 57. The fullest transcript of this remarkable discussion was published at the time in the *Rheinische Merkur*, no. 4, January 22, 2004: "Duell des Geistes," pp. 23–24.

168. Isaiah Berlin, "European Unity and Its Vicissitudes," in *The Crooked Timber of Humanity: Chapters in the History of Ideas* (London: John Murray, 1990), 175, 204.

169. Adam Smith, *The Theory of the Moral Sentiments* (Indianapolis: Liberty Fund, 1969), 264, 266, 271–72.

170. Ian Buruma and Avishai Margalit, *Occidentalism: The West in the Eyes of its Enemies* (New York: Penguin, 2004), 11.

171. "Funeral Presents Opportunity to Renew Diplomatic Contacts," *Financial Times*, April 8, 2005.

Index